MY COLLEGE FINANCE

A guide to understanding personal finance for students and parents

J.L. Thompson

GORILLA PUBLISHING

Although based on true stories, certain events in the book have been fictionalized for educational content and impact.

Cover and book design: Stacy Luecker
www.EssexGraphix.com

Cover photography: Renee Greer
www.FrozeInBeauty.com

Editor: Chandra Sparks Taylor
www.chandrasparkstaylor.com

Gorilla Publishing
1025 Veterans Memorial Highway, Suite 310-229
Mableton, Georgia 30126
www.gorillapublishing.org

Publisher's Cataloging In Publication—Pending

ISBN: 978-0-9796354-9-6
LCN: 2007902308

Printed in the United States of America

To Hattie K. Thomas aka The Old Girl.

Mom, I love you.

Acknowledgments

I would like to thank my best friend, confidante, and wife, Tanya Allford-Thompson. Thank you for continuously pushing me to pursue this dream and for not allowing me to make excuses for why I could not complete this book. To Ashley, Joaquin, Jr., and Nia Thompson, thank you for giving me continued support and drive to make this book a reality. I would also like to say a special thank you to all of my family, friends, and associates who have supported me through their words of encouragement and prayers.

To all of my fraternal brothers of Omega Psi Phi Fraternity, Inc., thank you for reminding me that everything must take place through a process and it is up to me to persevere in order to see it through.

To Karen Atkins at Unity of the Spirit publishing, thanks for the input on how to be a new writer without looking like a new writer. Thanks to Adrienne Starkey for editing my initial manuscript and for also giving me some insight into the book writing industry. Special thanks to Chandra Sparks Taylor of Taylor Editorial Service (www.chandrasparkstaylor.com) for educating me on the importance of having this book professionally edited. I also want to thank Chandra for all of her patience, insight, and guidance in this project. Thanks to Stacy Luecker of Essex Graphix (www.essexgraphix.com) for the awesome cover design and book layout. I really think we have a winner.

To Bobby Height at Career Sports & Entertainment, I really appreciate the guidance, brainstorming, and wisdom regarding all the potential marketing avenues available to college students worldwide.

And, finally, thanks to all the parents, educators, and students who have supported this book. It is my sincere hope that each of you will acquire financial knowledge from *My College Finance* that can and will be used for years to come. Thank you all.

TABLE OF CONTENTS

Preface

How do people learn about personal finance? This was the question I thought about for years, long before I even thought about writing a book on this topic. I looked back over my life from a personal finance perspective and really tried to pinpoint where and when I acquired the knowledge I have on this subject.

I was never taught about personal finance—I just gradually became more and more involved with it over time. One day I realized I was participating in a system that included checking accounts, credit cards, mortgages, loans, and investments, but I did not really know much about it.

In today's society, there is one item that has a significant impact on almost every aspect of an adult's livelihood. It's known as credit or creditworthiness. In our current economy, credit determines where people live, what type of car they drive, the accounts they can establish, and most important, where they work. Yes, credit can determine whether an individual is able to secure employment.

What is the primary goal for students going to college? Students attend an institute of higher learning to gain skills and specialized knowledge that will increase their chances for earning a living. If this is true, what happens when college students are not able to secure employment after investing thousands of dollars and years of education in undergraduate and graduate degrees? I will tell you what happens: disgust, embarrassment, or shame, and even worse, they do not understand what went wrong.

I also wrote this book for parents to have a resource of information that can help both high school and college students avoid personal finance pitfalls by increasing their financial literacy. The premise is that parents must understand personal finance, then and only then, will they be in a position to teach their children about it.

Many of my critics told me that high school and college students would not be interested in a book about personal finance. I disagree with them. I agree that many students may not be interested in this topic, but I wrote this book so the information will be available for those students seeking access to this information at a young age. Even if most students are not interested, their parents will be because they know the real-life consequences of not being financially literate.

This is why I spent the last two years of my life writing this book, because in today's economy, increased financial literacy is desperately needed among students as well as their parents worldwide. The three main objectives of this book are for students to achieve the following by the time they graduate from college:

1. Understand the basics of personal finance.
2. Improve financial literacy.
3. Learn how to effectively manage money and credit.

These three objectives, coupled with a college degree, will create a great foundation for any young person. If this book can help to shift the mind-set of the average student, they will have the potential to be in a much stronger financial position at an earlier age. I hope you enjoy the journey in this book and discover the things that will be critical to your financial success in life.

Introduction

Millions of high school and college students graduate every year and never receive any advice, knowledge, or wisdom regarding one of the most important aspects to their lives: personal finance. They are well versed on subject matter related to their majors, but the vast majority will leave school ill equipped to manage their new financial futures.

Today's students are establishing lines of credit much sooner than their parents' generation. Students are bombarded with everything from cell phones with pricey ring tones to unsecured credit cards as early as their sophomore year of high school. Colleges and universities across America allow cell phone companies, department stores and credit card companies to introduce their products to millions of unsuspecting students annually.

Credit card companies have an unfair advantage over the average high school or college student regarding the establishment of credit. The main goal of credit card companies is to get students to try their different products at an early age. The unfortunate part of this process is that these students—the majority of whom are college freshmen—do not have the necessary knowledge to make informed decisions about credit cards. More and more students are graduating with their degrees in one hand and large amounts of debt in the other. What is worse is that most college students do not have a clue how this debt, coupled with compromised credit histories, will immediately impact their lives after graduation.

College student enrollment is on the rise. There are roughly sixteen million students on college and university campuses nationwide. Take a moment and think about the potential financial and credit consequences of this current group. Based on data in the March 2005 issue of *Reader's Digest,* Americans' average outstanding credit card debt is $8,100-plus (not including student loans, car loans, housing costs, cellular bills, etc.). According to a six-week series entitled "Young and in Debt" that ran in *USA Today* during December 2006, the average college student owes around $5,700 in revolving debt, which includes credit card debt. In addition to this debt, students are also facing increasing amounts of student loan debt related to the rising cost of undergraduate and graduate education. Keep in mind that all of this debt will be well in place before graduates receive their first job offer.

Considering the above scenario, how long will it take the average student to pay off $5,700 of credit card debt? If they emulate the repayment patterns of their parents and pay the minimum amount due, it will take about ten years. Although many will not graduate with this much debt, some will have much higher balances that could take up to thirty years to pay off.

Today's college students are facing an economy that has never been seen before. Technology has made it easier for companies to prey on them through cable television, e-mail solicitations, cell phone solicitations, and the Internet. Students are bombarded with many opportunities to satisfy their need for instant gratification through the use of credit cards. By the time many of them (and their parents) realize the consequences of their credit decisions, it will be too late to avoid the financial hardships that lay ahead.

Hopefully, this book will become a trusted resource guide for students as well as their parents. The information contained in the following pages is essential for anyone who wants to protect themselves from the pitfalls of personal finance and credit-related issues. Many students prepare to various degrees for enrollment in college, but very few receive sound advice on how to increase their financial literacy related to personal finance. Let's explore the world of personal finance and credit among America's best and brightest students.

CHAPTER 1

Oblivious

*"The beginning of enlightenment
is to understand that you know nothing."*
—David Baird, author

February 13, 1987. I was in my junior year at Howard University in Washington, D.C., and it was my twentieth birthday. I was in the market for a present like a brand-new pair of Air Jordans, Timberland boots, or a Sony Walkman, which was new to the market. I went to an electronics store in the mall looking for the Walkman. Cassette tapes were big in the eighties, and I figured a Walkman would be a nice little gift to myself. Once I was ready to make my purchase, a store salesman asked me if I had seen the newest Walkman made by Sony. I told him that I had not, and he explained that it was a portable CD player instead of a cassette player. I asked the salesman for the price, and he responded it was on sale for $320. I told him that I did not have that kind of money to which he responded, "No problem."

The salesman asked me to apply for a store credit card in order to purchase the new Walkman. He explained that it would only take a few minutes to fill out the application and I could be instantly approved for a $500 store credit card. My first thought was, *Wow, I could get my very own credit card without the help of my parents.* The best part was that my parents would not have to know anything about it and would not have any input on what or how much I purchased. After I filled out the application, the salesman went to the rear of the store, and when he returned, he said the exact words we all like to hear: "You're approved."

I not only purchased the CD player but I also added five brand-new CDs. My birthday gift cost a whopping $438.97. This purchase marked the beginning or the birth of my credit life.

My first credit card statement arrived about a month later. The minimum amount due was $15. I thought, *This is cool. I have a new portable CD player with five of the hottest CDs, and I only have to pay $15 a month on my credit card bill.* The due date on the bill was not until the fifth of the following month, so I figured I had plenty of time to send in a payment. Days and weeks passed, but the $15 never made it to the mailbox.

The next month I received another bill for my credit card. The minimum amount due was $25, but the balance was $470.35. I was stunned at the increase from the previous month, especially since I had not made any new purchases. My first thought was that there was an error in my statement, so I called the credit card company to get my balance corrected.

I told the customer service representative that I had received my new bill and the balance was incorrect. I explained that I understood the $6.38 finance charge, but I did not understand how my balance had increased. I demanded that it be corrected immediately. The representative replied that the new balance was correct according to the company's files. She advised me that a $25 late fee had been added to my balance because no payment had been received for the last month's bill. *Twenty-five dollars.* I told her that was crazy. I became very upset with the representative because I felt like I had been deceived. I told her that the salesman at the store did not mention anything about a $25 late fee if I did not make a payment by a certain date. She laughed lightly, and I did not understand her reaction. She asked if I had read the terms and conditions of the agreement when I applied for the store card. Who reads the terms of a credit card agreement? I just wanted to know if I was approved. I reluctantly answered, "No" and stated that I had filled out my name, address, Social Security number, and phone number and signed it. The representative told me that I really needed to read the fine print in order to understand my rights and responsibilities, including guidelines for proper use. (See The Fine Print in Appendix D.) I apologized for my behavior and promised to make all my future payments on time. Since I had already been dinged with this thing called a late fee, I decided I'd better send my payment immediately. My payments were on time for the next three or four months, and then my bill-paying habits became out of sync again. Within a short period my balance was more than $645. I tried to start making my monthly payments of $25 again, but my balance was still going up.

I called the customer service department again to find out why my balance was slowly increasing instead of decreasing. This time the representative told me that my balance continued to increase because of over-the-limit fees. The representative advised me this fee is charged when the balance on the account is higher than the credit limit. She stated that a $30 fee was added to my bill each month that my balance was higher than my credit limit. My minimum ($25) payment was going toward the over-the-limit fee, and the finance charges continued to increase my balance.

When I finally understood the fees related to the department store credit card, my balance was $671. I remember asking myself, *How did my balance go from $437 to $671 in such a short period?*

My first lesson in dealing with credit was very expensive. I learned the hard way that credit cards must be managed in a responsible way to avoid additional costs. If I did not know any better, I would have sworn that this system was set up to make money on unsuspecting students like me.

According to Robert Manning, a noted credit card industry expert, late fees rose from $1.7 billion in 1996 to $7.7 billion in 2003. The way the system is designed, a large portion of the profits are made in late, over-the-limit, and finance fees, not in credit card purchases.

Millions of America's best and brightest are introduced to this system every year at a very young age, the majority during their freshman year of college. Yet most of these young students are not adequately prepared to understand the "real" credit card system. The unfortunate part of this phenomenon is that millions of students have become financially trapped in this system and many will not recover for several years after college. To all the students and parents who are reading this information for the first time: Welcome to America…where capitalism is our chosen way of life.

Learning Points for Students and Parents

- Take time to read and understand the terms and conditions of any credit card agreement.
- Learn about finance charges, annual fees, late fees, over-the-limit fees, etc.
- If your balance exceeds your credit limit, be sure to make extra payments as soon as possible to bring the balance below your credit limit.

- Develop the habit of paying off your entire balance every month to avoid finance charges and penalties.
- Remember, credit card purchases are not free. Charges must be repaid with money (cash).
- Be responsible with your credit accounts.

CHAPTER 2

The Birth of Credit

"In every aspect of our lives, we are always asking ourselves, How am I of value? What is my worth? Yet I believe that worthiness is our birthright."
—Oprah Winfrey

When women become pregnant, it usually takes forty weeks from the day of conception for them to give birth. During this time, a baby goes through a series of developmental stages, each of which is extremely important to the final outcome of a healthy newborn. If the baby is born too early, serious problems can arise such as birth defects or even death. If the baby is not delivered once it is fully matured, complications can also arise if it is allowed to stay in the womb. There are precise developmental stages to anything that is produced naturally that will signal when the object is mature and ready for birth.

Here is a little known fact about credit in relation to college students. Most students initially establish or give birth to credit between the ages of seventeen and twenty-three. Unlike everything else that develops in nature, there is no development stage for students when they begin to establish credit. Once they realize they have instant access to credit, many will get new cards as soon as possible if not sooner. They do not give any thought to the fact that credit should be developed in a series of stages. When credit is not developed properly, serious problems arise such as negative credit (bad credit), impulse purchases, collection accounts, and even withdrawal from school due to increased credit card debts.

Students who develop too much credit card debt too rapidly may be forced to withdraw from school. This occurs because students or their parents are not able to pay all the credit card bills in addition to current college costs. Unpaid credit card debt can also lead to the development of collection accounts, which are created when credit card lenders are unable to get students or parents to repay card charges. When bills go unpaid for a period of time—usually three to six months—lenders transfer accounts to collection companies.

Unlike credit card companies, collection companies' sole purpose of existence is to collect debts. These companies will use a variety of tactics that include multiple calls, threatening letters or harassing communications in order to collect on past-due accounts. Many college students feel they have to endure these tactics because they do not want their parents to know they have created so much credit card debt. Unfortunately, there have been documented cases of suicide among college students linked to the pressure of credit card debts.

Just as there are things that are good and bad for pregnant women, there are certain things that students can do to help ensure good development of their new credit. Here are some of the things that have a positive impact on credit:

- Gain knowledge of proper use of credit before applying for the first card or account.

- Solicit input from parents before establishing credit.
- Consistently pay all bills on time.
- Keep credit card balances at 50% or less of the available card limit. This will help improve your credit score.
- Do not exceed the credit limit.
- Do not establish more than two credit card accounts while in college. No exceptions.
- Avoid multiple applications for credit. Multiple applications for new credit can have a negative effect on credit. It will also increase the probability of increased credit card debt.
- Keep all bills current.
- Never close accounts once paid in full because this will decrease your credit score.
- Develop and maintain credit accounts for a minimum of twenty-four months.
- Installment accounts are an excellent option for establishing credit (i.e., electronics store, furniture store, jewelry store, etc.)

Let's also quickly examine things that have a negative impact on credit:

- Default on student loans.
- Late payments of student loans.
- Any collection accounts.
- Late or missed payments.
- Establishment of multiple credit accounts in less than sixty days.
- Maxed-out credit accounts—spending to the limit.
- Over-the-limit accounts.
- Closed paid-off accounts, which cause credit scores to decline.

- Not making timely payments or infrequent payments. This is known as slow credit.
- Transferring credit card debt among different cards. (e.g., transferring credit card balances to a card with a lower interest rate.) This is known as credit surfing.
- Purchasing items on credit for friends.

Establishing and maintaining credit is a lifelong financial skill that all students and parents need to learn and master over time. There appears to be a simple formula for developing a good credit history—pay bills on time, keep credit card balances low, manage accounts, etc. The truth is that establishing and maintaining good credit can be as challenging as losing weight, quitting smoking, or creating financial success. With each of these examples, following simple steps consistently will achieve the desired outcome.

The Ability to Focus

Some students or their parents do not exhibit the self-discipline to create and consistently strive for certain goals. Many people need an external driving force to assist them (e.g., personal trainer to lose weight). The same is true for finance. Many people need that external driving force but neglect to ask for help. Students should solicit help from their parents and financial educators to get additional insight or strategies related to credit. Students can also make a commitment to increase their financial literacy through the Internet, books, magazines, and newspapers.

Without discipline, people always will struggle with their credit. Good credit shows that an individual has developed the discipline to control his personal desires over time. Some call it delayed gratification or the ability to say no to excessive spending, pretentious needs, and the desire to "keep up with the Joneses."

When there is a lack of discipline, there is a constant need to satisfy personal desires, not personal necessities. Therefore, when people establish good credit, their ability to have more "things" automatically increases. When the ability to get more things increases, so does the urge to fulfill more desires. Ironically, acquiring these "things" typically causes credit scores to decrease. This is a cyclical process that continues over a person's lifetime until self-control is developed.

Students must understand that in order to become the masters of their own fate, it is paramount that they learn the rules of credit. Today's students are living in the information age, and each day they want and need more items to maintain a certain standard of living. The ability to acquire all these wants and needs is directly linked to creditworthiness.

If students and parents take their time to make sure that credit is developed gradually, they will have a better chance of creating improved credit outcomes in the future. Students should be reminded that there is no rush—this is a life-long process, so take your time to learn the lessons of credit.

CHAPTER 3

It's All About Your Credit

*"The only good is knowledge
and the only evil is ignorance."*
—Socrates

The majority of students who acquire new credit lines each year do not understand the real impact on their futures. Most of these students establish credit lines for unsecured credit cards, department store cards, cell phones, etc., not out of necessity, but by choice. A 2006 Experian credit services survey of three million twenty-somethings reported that their average amount of debt was $20,000 or more. If a college student has $20,000 worth of debt as an undergraduate, how much more will he accumulate the first five years after graduation? Not only are students graduating with increased debt, the worst part is that many of them will also develop bad credit.

When students are going through their college years, the last thing on their mind is credit. However, it is the one area that will be critical to a student's well-being, no matter which major he chooses to study. The American economy is rapidly changing, and cash has taken a backseat to credit. During the industrial and agricultural ages, cash was king. Now that we are in the information age, credit is the premier component that determines a person's quality of life.

Students who are unaware or unconcerned about their creditworthiness will find it difficult to get established after their college years. More and more service industries (e.g., housing, car insurance, cable, life insurance, banking, etc.) are requiring that individuals have a certain level of creditworthiness in order to be approved for services. Many college students who do not understand the impact of creditworthiness in today's society will be limited in the goods and services they will be able to acquire. Negative or compromised credit will essentially create a class of young adults who will be locked out of many of life's opportunities.

This pattern of behavior develops simply because students have not been properly prepared to manage money or credit. In addition to this, students do not understand the significance of negative credit. From preschool through high school, today's students are taught the basic fundamentals needed to be successful in college. They learn more advanced subjects such as world literature, algebra, and foreign languages by the age of twelve. Students often receive this information both at school and at home. The average student attends school about eight hours per day, which amounts to about 1,500 hours per school year. All of this time is utilized to ensure that students are familiar with the academic skills needed to be successful in both college and in life.

In contrast to all of the years of academic preparation, college students have received very little, if any, instruction on the subjects of personal finance and credit management. Many students have unsecured credit cards, major department store cards, and cell phone accounts by their eighteenth birthdays. Can a student be successful in college courses if he never learned to read or write? If your answer is no, why do we expect kids to be successful in personal finance or credit management without any prior knowledge or preparation? Lack of knowledge is the basis for why students do not know how to manage their personal finances and credit. Without this knowledge, they fall victim to a system that will impact their personal and professional lives for many years.

Some critics have said that it is parents' responsibility to educate their children about credit and personal finance. The problem with this theory is that parents can only teach their children what they know. If parents have limited information on these subjects, they cannot responsibly pass this information on to their children. Unfortunately, many of these parents have not been properly educated on the topics of credit and personal finance nor do they care to learn. Therefore, they experience challenges with their own personal finances, including credit.

Many parents unknowingly teach their children about personal finance and credit through their own daily activities. If parents are guilty of mismanaging their credit and income—late or slow payments, disconnect notices, overdue bills, calls from bill collectors, and bankruptcies or repossessions—students are at risk to develop these same habits. When students see their parents mishandling their financial obligations, they get the wrong impression on how personal finance and credit should be developed and maintained.

The reality is that millions of students will graduate from college financially illiterate regarding personal finance and credit. After graduation many of these students will receive a rude awakening to the power of credit in the real world.

Learning Points for Students and Parents

- A student's creditworthiness will determine which goods/services he will be able to acquire.
- The average amount of debt for college graduates is $20,000 or more.
- In today's economy, credit is more valuable than cash.
- Schools must start to help educate students on the importance of creditworthiness.
- Lack of knowledge is the primary reason students develop large amounts of credit card debt at an early age.
- Millions of students graduate from college annually financially illiterate.

CHAPTER 4

Understanding the Power of Credit

"I'm worth about $400 million in cash, but I'm worth about $4 billion in credit."
—Donald Trump, real estate mogul

Students are constantly reminded from an early age that the most important factor related to success in school is a good grade point average. In today's world, the most important factor in determining how successful a person becomes is more strongly linked to his credit profile. It is very important that students begin to learn the meaning of credit, including the fundamentals needed to manage accounts, as young adults.

Credit is defined as faith, reputed integrity, transfer of goods sold on trust with confidence of future payment, and time given for payment of goods sold on trust. Simply stated, credit is one's ability to purchase items (real estate, cars, furniture, etc.) with the expectation to pay for them in the near future.

Long before the first credit card was issued, individuals possessed credit. Once students understand credit and how it functions in today's economy, this information will become priceless.

College students are the only group of credit applicants who do not have to qualify in the traditional manner to receive a credit card. The only criteria college students must meet is to be actively enrolled in any college or university. This exception to traditional credit requirements is an excellent opportunity for students to build a solid credit history.

Young adults who are not enrolled in college have to qualify for a credit card according to traditional guidelines. This includes having an acceptable credit history and income verification in order to be approved. It is more difficult for these young adults to get approved if they do not have qualifying income or established credit histories right out of high school. If students establish good credit habits while they are still in college, they will have more financial opportunities after graduation.

Establishing good credit in today's society can be a very powerful tool when used correctly. Used in the right way, credit can assist students in taking advantage of items like low interest rate mortgages or credit cards and even no interest auto loans.

The ability to secure low interest or no interest loans will put college students in a greater financial position as they transition into the independence of adulthood. Students who develop good credit histories will have the ability to purchase a primary residence (home, town house, or condo) while in school. They can also purchase rental property, making income off their investment. Either decision would put students in a position to generate money. All this can be done by leveraging good credit to obtain financing to purchase assets. Robert Kiyosaki, author of the best-selling book *Rich Dad Poor Dad,* defines an asset as any item that puts money in your pocket.

This means college students could have the ability to control a $100,000 asset with little or none of their own money invested. This is the same process Donald Trump uses when he takes on a new $600 million real estate project. He may put some of his own money in the deal, but the vast majority of it comes from the bank. This is possible because Donald Trump has established good credit with several financial institutions. The average college student may not become the next Donald Trump, but if he creates a strong enough credit history, he will have access to things that are reserved for a select group of disciplined individuals. Remember American Express' motto, membership has its privileges.

Many students will not be able to purchase a vehicle, lease an apartment, buy a home, or establish utilities in their name. In some cases, these students will be forced to use sub-prime financial institutions that charge very high interest rates for auto or home loans. These rates translate into high monthly payments, which constrain a new graduate's finances. High interest rates and high monthly payments help to create a financial situation that will eventually entrap them. College students must understand that negative credit histories have the ability to affect their well-being for several years.

Credit and Employment

There is a new credit implication affecting millions of college students, but very few are even aware of this new practice. An increasing amount of employers have started to review credit reports of potential applicants. This process has serious consequences for college graduates. Prospective employers have started using credit reports to make determinations regarding hiring. During the recruiting process for new hires, a college student's creditworthiness has become equally as important as a good GPA. In addition to credit histories, potential employers are also concerned about how much personal debt a new college graduate has accumulated.

Employers review these credit reports to ensure that students have a positive history handling their own finances. Students who have too much personal debt or delinquent payment histories will most likely be excluded for employment consideration. Many employers feel that if a student cannot manage his own finances, he cannot sufficiently work with corporate finances. This type of corporate standard is rapidly becoming the norm as opposed to the exception.

Millions graduate from college and universities every spring, but many of their employment opportunities will be affected by their credit histories. Since the use of credit review by employers is such a new practice, many students will not even be aware when they are affected. Typically if a student is notified that he was not offered a position, the rationale for the company's decision is not included.

Many students will be left to ponder the reasons. Instead of thinking, *Did I wear the right outfit? Was my GPA high enough? Did I interview well?*, now students have to ask more relevant questions: *Did I have an acceptable credit history? Do I have too much credit card or personal debt?*

Students need to always remember why they chose to attend college: increased employment potential, ability to obtain a skill that will provide a lifetime of income or the opportunity to gain an advanced level of specialized knowledge. All of these are great reasons to pursue college or advanced degrees, but equally important students need to be aware that bad credit can devalue their degree or severely limit their academic aspirations.

Learning Points for Students and Parents

- College students can qualify for credit without income or credit history.
- Good credit can create increased financial opportunities.

- Establishing good credit will be a financial advantage to students, e.g., low/no interest loans.
- Students or parents should purchase a home, condominium or townhouse as soon as possible to establish equity.
- Negative credit histories may have a direct impact on potential employment opportunities.
- Students need to learn how to leverage good credit.
- Bad or negative credit can devalue a college degree.
- Stay focused on your future after college.

DOLLARS AND SENSE

One out of five college students will accumulate $10,000 or more credit card debt prior to graduation.

CHAPTER 5

To Owe or Not to Owe

"Creditors have better memories than debtors."
—Benjamin Franklin

While students are in college, debt is rarely a topic of conversation. Although more students now require loans to complete their education, very few give any real thought to their future debts after college. If students elect to further their education by attending graduate or professional school, the amount of proposed debt can be staggering. The reality of these debts usually arrives in the form of a loan payment coupon booklet about six months after graduation. Once students realize they must begin making payments on these debts, they ask the infamous question, "How am I going to pay all these bills?"

DOLLARS AND SENSE

The U.S. trade deficit for 2006 is estimated to be $425 billion. This means the United States will consume $425 billion more than we produce.

The first step students must take in addressing their bills is to develop an effective budget. Students should create a list of all their bills, the amount owed, due dates, and the balance using a spreadsheet. Once they have listed all of this information, they should total each column. This will give them insight into exactly how much debt they currently have as well as their total monthly obligations. Hopefully, this will help them avoid unnecessary late fees and penalties for slow or non-payments.

Account	Monthly Payments	Due Date Payments	Annual
Cell Phone	$80	1/15/07	$960
The Gap	$20	1/26/07	$240
Best Buy	$25	1/7/07	$300
Visa	$50	1/8/07	$600
MasterCard	$50	1/20/07	$600
Electric	$70	1/20/07	$840
Natural Gas	$75	1/15/07	$900
Water	$40	1/17/07	$480
Cable	$50	1/23/07	$600
Phone/DSL	$100	1/22/07	$1,200
Student Loan	$175	1/20/07	$2,100
Rent	$700	1/1/07	$8,400
Car Loan	$300	1/10/07	$3,600
TOTALS	**$1,735**		**$20,820**

The above table illustrates what the average student's debts could look like immediately following college. In addition to debts, students need to know how much income they will have each month, semester, or school year. This will help them figure out if they have a surplus or deficit. When students discover they have more income than their expenses, this is known as a surplus. When expenses are more than income, this is known as a deficit. If students find they have a deficit, this should be a red flag that their current expenses need to be decreased or income increased. If they find they have a surplus of money after all of their expenses are paid, they should deposit it into a savings or investment account. While students are in undergraduate or graduate school, little thought is given to depositing any extra money into a savings or investment account. According to a research study by Harrell marketing group, college students in 2005 had a collective buying power of $200 billion. It was estimated that the average college student had between $660 and $1,100 in monthly disposable income.

Remember, this is just an example. Many students will graduate with far greater debts, and some will have a lower amount. In this example, this student would be responsible for repaying annual debts totaling $20,820 with monthly payments of $1,735, which does not seem to be very large, but let's consider a few factors that would make this more significant:

Fact #1: Many students who graduate from college may not find adequate employment within the first six months to a year after leaving school.

Fact #2: Many students return home to live with their parents after graduation, but their parents are not fully aware of the student's bills. Therefore, it is not uncommon for some or all of these bill payments to be paid late or not at all. In addition to living at home, students may still be unemployed.

Fact #3: Many new graduates actually get decent jobs and can afford their first apartment/condo/home soon after graduation. Based on historical spending patterns, these new "independent" graduates will accumulate even more debt (e.g., new furniture, trips, car accessories, home electronics, etc.) faster than students in the first two examples.

The common thread with all three of the above facts is that in each case the $1,735 monthly obligation has the potential to entrap these students for several years. Students who fall into the first group (Fact #1) may not have adequate income to support their monthly obligations because they are unemployed. Therefore, they may pay their bills sporadically, if they pay at all. This will significantly affect the student's credit rating. Also, due to all the fees associated with these debts, it will ultimately cost students much more to pay off these debts.

Students who fall into the second group (Fact #2) will have similar problems. Although they have moved back home with their parents, this may not have any bearing on their debts. Students at this age feel they are adults and their bills are personal. If they do not find adequate employment, they may experience the same fate as the students in the first group. These students' parents may have the added financial burden of "helping" to pay for their children's newly acquired debt. Many parents may find that after paying for years of college tuition, they are not in a financial position to assist with repaying more debts.

Students who fall into the third group (Fact #3) are at the highest risk because they have income and they are living on their own. This independent living is not the problem, it is the fact that these young adults have access to new employment income. With their salary, these new graduates tend to increase their debt load faster than the previous two groups because they view their newfound income as limitless. It is not unusual for them to purchase new cars, wardrobes, furniture, and vacations. Also, these students tend to get offers to increase their credit limits since they now have reportable payroll income.

Many of these young adults will accumulate a substantial amount of debt in a short period of time. Their general feeling regarding these new obligations is, "I will pay for it when the bill comes." The problem with this mentality is that new graduates do not understand how long it normally takes to pay off these types of debts. The *Atlanta Journal Constitution* reported in an April 2006 article that it would take twenty-six years to pay off a $5,000 credit card balance at 17% interest, making minimum monthly payments of $121. In many instances, it could take as long as thirty years to pay off some of these newly created debts. All college students must keep in mind that they cannot afford to create a large amount of debt before they graduate because their future income is not guaranteed.

Students who leave school and develop the habit of making slow, missed, or no payments toward monthly obligations will find out the meaning of financial discrimination. This type of discrimination will not be based on their race, religion, gender, or sexual preference, but rather what is perceived as their lack of a proven record of consistent bill payments. Once students are placed into this category, life can get really hard.

Think about how these students will feel when they are faced with the reality that they can't lease an apartment, buy a house or condo, purchase a car, or more importantly they get turned down for their first job. Many students and parents may think this is an overstatement, but consider that there are an increasing number of college students returning home to live with their parents after graduation. There are many reasons for this trend, but one of the biggest is that more and more students are not in a position to financially establish themselves after college. When students find out they cannot qualify to get their own house or apartment or they can't get their utilities connected, where do they turn? Typically, Mom and Dad. Without acceptable credit, being independent can be extremely challenging for new graduates.

College students who have been educated in how to play the credit game leave school in a very advantageous position. Another emerging trend among new college graduates is the purchase of houses, condos, and town houses instead of leasing apartments. Owning property at a young age puts new graduates in a powerful financial position.

It is widely known that most real estate will appreciate in value over time. As this happens, these new graduates will benefit from the value of their property in the form of equity in their property. Historically, real estate will appreciate 3% to 5% annually, depending on the region of the country. Once students are ready to sell their property, they will receive the accumulated equity in the form of cash. This financial position is much better compared to renting an apartment for several years after graduation.

When students rent apartments, they receive zero financial benefits from the accumulated money spent on rent. In contrast, students who purchase a home, condo, town house, etc., will benefit financially from their monetary investment in the form of mortgage payments. These payments will decrease the outstanding principal amount owed on the property, which typically continues to increase in value and translates into increased equity. Mortgage payments also create tax advantages because the interest portion of the mortgage payment is tax deductible. Buying property right out of college is a new wealth-building principal that can be executed by students who have developed and maintained acceptable creditworthiness.

DOLLARS AND SENSE

Cash generated from a home's appreciation and subsequent sale can be used to offset college debt, including student loans and credit card debt.

College graduates who have the ability to maintain acceptable credit, secure income, and purchase homes are less likely to return to live with their parents. These students can become self-reliant faster than their fellow graduates who have difficulty getting established financially. Students with good or acceptable credit can get health insurance, auto loans, auto insurance, etc., which help them become financially independent of their parents.

Learning Points for Students and Parents

- Students must learn how to create an effective budget.
- Students need to know the difference between a surplus and a deficit.
- Students with a deficit need to decrease expenses and increase their income (e.g. part-time job).
- Students with a surplus should establish an investment (mutual fund) or savings account to deposit excess money.
- Many college graduates will not secure employment for six months to a year following graduation.
- An increasing number of college graduates are returning home to live with parents because of increased amounts of debt.
- Owning property at an early age will create a powerful financial position for new college graduates.
- College graduates who maintain acceptable credit, secure employment income and purchase property are less likely to return home to live with their parents.

CHAPTER 6

Rusty's Story

"Gambling promises the poor
what property performs for the rich—
something for nothing."
—George Bernard Shaw

The following is a true story that shows why it's important to take advantage of good credit, money management, and income as an undergraduate college student. While still an undergraduate, Floyd Long, Jr., aka Rusty was able to leverage advice from his parents and good personal finance skills to make a life-changing decision. He was able to purchase a piece of real estate at an early age, which has continued to pay him financial benefits for more than sixteen years. This is his true story.

Making Money

In 1986, my sophomore year at Howard University, I started working for the Department of Defense at the Office of Naval

Research as a student worker. I could work up to twenty hours a week for slightly over minimum wage. My first assignment was in the mailroom. It gave me the opportunity to learn the players in the organization. I proved myself, and I was recommended for a transfer to the computer room. Although the transfer involved no increase in salary, the reassignment allowed me to learn about mainframe computer operation. Once again, the managers in the computer room saw my work ethic and mentored me. When I expressed my desire to take one of the vacant full-time contractor positions, they gave me the recommendation. In 1987, I accepted a full-time position with Technology Applications Incorporated (TAI), a minority government contractor. My starting salary was $21,000. That was good money at the time, but the true benefit was that TAI paid a portion (80%) of my tuition. Once I accepted the full-time position, my older coworkers advised me to join the federal credit union to take advantage of all of its benefits. I promised my parents I would not drop out of college. In my mind, being a full-time employee and a full-time student meant partying part-time. I had to make it work.

The Property Search

Before the purchase of my condo, I was crashing with my sister in her rented apartment in Northern Virginia. She was a recent Howard University graduate and was working her first full-time job. During that time, she was looking to purchase a home. I went with her to see countless properties and learned some basic real estate lingo. While helping my sister search for her potential new home, I was exposed to several areas of the home-buying process such as down payment assistance, closing cost, fair market value, etc. Midstream in her property search, she changed courses and decided to pursue a law degree. This meant that she would be a full-time student, and she did not feel comfortable taking on property debt. I knew the benefit of ownership as well as the bottomless pit of renting during my college years. I was able to pick up the property search.

During my search, I also saw a lot of properties, which varied from condos to single-family homes in Washington, DC, Virginia, and Maryland. Some of the prices scared me, but I was determined to own something. During my search, I got a lot of advice from my sister and my father. I knew that my parents would have to continue to advise me as well as help me out financially if necessary. I stayed in contact with them every step of the process. After I found a property I liked, one of the best pieces of advice my father gave me was to wait until my condo purchase was complete before I bought a new car I wanted very badly.

The Purchase

I found the perfect place in 1988. It was a two-bedroom, two-bathroom foreclosed condo, owned by a bank. It was centrally located to Howard University and my sister's new law school. I was looking more to the amenities: central A/C, walkout patio, a parking space, and a view of the community pool. Later, I recognized some intangible selling points: close to four other colleges, new appliances, new carpet, and on a bus line to the subway and downtown Washington, DC. I later learned that the property was discounted to sell quickly and the bank paid a share of the closing cost because banks are not in the business of owning property.

The purchasing process was foreign to me. I'll admit now that I had a poker face, but I was scared. I filled out the application and committed to the purchase. I was always frugal by nature. Since I had started working full time, I established credit through the Naval Federal Credit Union. My credit encompassed a used car loan and a credit card with a $500 limit. My lender told me that my income and good credit allowed me to purchase the condo without a cosigner, My mortgage was through a first-time home buyer's program that had a low interest loan. Since the closing cost and the down payment cleaned out my savings, my sister went to my closing and served as my pro bono lawyer, even though she was a first-year law student.

The Payoff

I was a twenty-year-old homeowner. At the time, I truly did not know what I had pulled off. I think I was more focused on not letting my family down. My sister and I moved in with the agreement that I would pay the mortgage and she would pay the maintenance fee, which included the utilities. This translated into a 60/40 split of the expenses, which was less than renting an equivalent apartment or campus housing. We moved in with the free help of my friends.

After my sister finished law school, she relocated to Georgia. I lived in the condo for five years through graduate school. After that, I accepted a position in my field and relocated to New York City, even though I was fearful of having two mortgage payments. Since that time, I have rented the condo through word of mouth to family and friends. Because of the location, price, and amenities, it has never been vacant. In 2008, the condo will be paid off. One of those same friends who helped me move in is a real estate agent in Maryland. I asked him to run some property price comparisons in my condominium complex. The value of my property has increased more than 400% since the original purchase. I will likely hold on to the condo for the near future and continue to build equity.

Advice

Today's college students should put their energies into multi-tasking. By that I mean most of these students are young, single, and have enough energy to establish a financial foundation that will benefit them in the future. They should combine their income and credit to purchase property such as a condo, town house, or single-family home, which will allow them to start to build equity. The odds of creating wealth through the use of real estate are increased when students make their purchase at an early age. Historically, real estate values have increased over time, especially when property has been held for at least ten years or more. These increased values can be converted into profit income if the property is later sold and the proceeds can be used to pay off college costs such as student loans or credit card debt. Homeownership is a powerful concept to which students should be exposed as early as possible.

Rusty's Key Advice

- Plan your lifestyle before you purchase—control spending habits and establish a budget.
- Research. Speak to family/friends who are homeowners, research your local real estate market for prices, terminology, and mortgage terms.
- Establish and maintain a good credit score. Creditworthiness influences mortgage terms and other decisions (e.g., insurance, employment).
- Become a homeowner instead of a real estate investor. Purchase a property in which you can live. Speculative "flip" properties require investment capital and knowledge of the real estate market a student may not have.

CHAPTER 7

Understanding Interest

"Interest, you're either paying it or you're earning it."
—Hearn Dukes, financier

Interest is the best friend of the wealthy and the worst enemy of everyone else. It is known in the financial world to be a silent killer to an individual's financial health. The average person is constantly losing money through interest, but they seldom realize the true financial impact over time. Wealthy individuals love interest because it is additional money they receive when they make wise investments.

Interest is an extra charge that is added to the principal balance, also known as the original loan amount borrowed by an individual. When the principal amount of the loan is repaid, the borrower is also required to pay interest (extra money) in addition to the original loan. This is why college students who graduate with $50,000 in student loans will most likely repay twice that amount when interest is added to their payments.

The average person has little or limited knowledge of how interest works in relation to personal finance. Banks, credit card companies, and student loan companies all structure their loans or extensions of credit to take advantage of interest. These loans are designed to have various rates depending on a student's credit score. Students who have poor credit are required to have their parents co-sign for their student loan. When parents have poor credit, the student will still be eligible for the loan, but it could be at the highest interest rate allowed. Historically student loans offered interest rates as low as 3%, but as of July 1, 2006, rates increased to as much as 20%.

Some companies will refer to interest as "finance charges," which is often synonymous with interest charges because the focus is the same to the lending institution. The creation of additional income by adding interest charges to the principal outstanding balance for any loan or extension of credit.

Students who start to accumulate debt at an early age do not understand the silent impact of interest charges. All consumer loans, department store cards, credit cards, as well as any personal loans from a lending institution will have interest charges attached to the principal amount of the debt. Interest charges are one way that creditors continue to add to the outstanding balance even though consumers may be making timely minimum monthly payments. If the interest charge exceeds the payment amount due, the outstanding balance will continue to increase.

For example, if the interest rate on a $1,000 debt is 24.9%, the monthly amount of interest charged would be about $21. Now, if the minimum monthly payment is $10, the account balance would actually increase to $1,011 after the payment has been made because the interest charge was $21, but the minimum monthly payment was only $10. Therefore, there is $11 left over from the interest charge that was not paid. This portion of the interest charge will be added to the original amount of $1,000.

Meanwhile, the interest will continue to make the outstanding balance slowly increase over time.

This type of bill-paying pattern can go on for years because individuals feel they are paying their bills on time. Although this is true, they are not paying enough toward the principle balance every month to significantly decrease the original amount of the debt.

DOLLARS AND SENSE

All payments made on credit cards/loans will go toward interest charges first, then the remainder of the payment will be applied to the principal amount of the debt.

Credit card companies intentionally set up accounts in this manner to encourage individuals to only make minimum monthly payments on their outstanding balances. In the early nineties, the minimal amount required for credit card payments were based on 5% of the outstanding balance. Credit card companies were making huge profits from the interest, but they wanted more. A strategy was developed that would increase their profits from interest charges by extending the amount of time it would take consumers to pay off their credit card balances. The required minimal payment was decreased from 5% to 2% of the outstanding credit card balance. Consumers were pleased with the decrease, but they were not aware that they would be paying significantly more interest with the extended payments.

Other industries such as mortgages, auto loans, and student loans adopted similar strategies to increase their revenues. The forty-year mortgage, seventy-two-month auto loan and the forty-year student loan repayment plan were created to lower consumers' monthly payments by extending the repayment period. This strategy has created billions in additional revenue for each of these industries, and consumers have remained in debt longer. Consumers think lower monthly payments are more affordable, but the reality is that these payments prolong the time it takes to completely eliminate debts.

Most high-priced items such as houses, cars, motorcycles, furniture, high priced electronics, etc., are purchased through financing, meaning a loan is established for the full purchase price or some portion thereof for the desired item. As the loan is repaid over a specified period, interest is added into the payments. In the early stages of the loan, most of the monthly payment is applied to the interest charge, with a small portion being applied to the principal balance. This ensures that the lending institution will receive all of the interest charged before any of the original loan amount starts to decrease. Slow or missed payments for items purchased through financing can dramatically increase the total amount required to pay off the original debt.

The following story is a good example of how interest and finance charges work in the real world.

The Real World

John, a recent graduate of State University, responds to an ad in his local newspaper regarding special automotive financing for new college graduates. He goes down to a local car dealership and picks out a brand-new sports utility vehicle, priced at $23,000. Once he has chosen his SUV, the salesman helps him decide on which accessories he would like to add (e.g., alloy wheels, undercoating, extended warranty, etc.). Once all of the amenities are added, the final price is $25,000. John mentions that he is a new college graduate and would like the special finance rate of 1.9% APR (annual percentage rate) advertised in the newspaper. The salesman assures John that he should be eligible for this special promotion.

The salesman asks John if he would like to take his new truck for a test drive. John replies, "Sure. Where are the keys?" The salesman hands John the keys and tells him to drive the truck over the weekend. John is shocked. "You mean I can drive it for the weekend for free?"

"Sure, just let me know how it drives on Monday," the salesman replies.

Early Monday morning John returns to the dealership. He tells the salesman that the truck is great and that all of his friends love it. He says that he is ready to buy the truck and has a $1,000 for the down payment. When John finally sits down with the sales manager, he is advised that the interest rate for his truck purchase was based on his current credit score. The sales manager tells John that according to his credit report, he has had some recent late payments on his accounts. Therefore, the best interest rate he can offer John is 14%.

Although John doesn't understand the impact of the 14% interest rate on his truck purchase, he agrees to the loan at the higher interest rate. The sales manager tells John that his monthly payments will be $468. John thinks, *That's expensive, but I deserve it.* The sales manager tells John that his payments will be made monthly over the next seventy-two months. The amount financed is $25,000 and the total amount paid after all the monthly payments will be $41,180. The interest paid on this loan will be $16,180. John agrees to all of the terms of the purchase, signs the necessary paperwork, and leaves very excited about his new truck.

DOLLARS AND SENSE

Students and parents must learn to understand how interest works with regard to purchases using credit or loans.

From the above example, students should start to understand that it is not what you buy, it's how much it's going to cost you in the long run. Students should be aware that when high-ticket items are financed, all of the interest (in John's case, $16,180) will be recovered or repaid first. This means that the first thirty-six of seventy-two payments will go directly to the interest charges. Once these have been paid, the remainder of the payments will be applied toward the principal amount of the purchase (in the example, $25,000).

This information may seem straightforward, but very few students are aware of this process. Most individuals never fully understand how financing works, therefore they continue to make the same mistakes throughout their lifetime. Once an individual understands how interest works, he can implement ways to minimize finance charges. The moral of the story is to understand what you are buying and how much it is going to cost you now and in the future.

Sound financial advice for college students purchasing new automobiles is to buy the car they really like, keep the vehicle without trading it, and pay off the loan as soon as possible. Students will benefit if they keep the same car and pay off the loan as opposed to trading the car in for a new one. Paying off an auto loan and keeping an existing vehicle will help students generate additional income by eliminating their monthly auto loan payment. The money that would typically be paid on a car note can be applied to other debts such as student loans or credit card bills to eliminate those more quickly. Another strategy would be to make monthly deposits into an investment account equal to the previous car payment. The investment will have the ability to earn interest which would help to increase the total amount of the investment. This would be a positive way to benefit from interest.

Credit cards, student loans and auto loans take a certain amount of time to repay with the interest attached to it. None of us can predict what will happen with employment or income over the next five to seven years. If students come out of college and enter into a long-term obligation (seventy-two months/six years) like a car loan, they often do not realize they are spending income that has not been produced. If the economy declines, a company closes, or if there are layoffs, they run the risk of not being able to pay this obligation. We must be very smart and cautious when entering into long-term financial commitments because we never know what the future holds.

In the real world, students as well as their parents will finance high-ticket items such as cars, houses, or expensive electronics. The following are some strategies to minimize the amount of interest paid on these items:

- Do not purchase high-ticket items on impulse. Research and plan these purchases.
- Save money to make a large down payment or pay cash for automobiles.
- Make payments more often than monthly (e.g., weekly or biweekly). Frequent payments will reduce the outstanding principal. Therefore, interest charges are reduced because interest is calculated on the outstanding principal balance.
- Finance cars for forty-eight months or less.
- Do not purchase houses, town houses, or condos with forty-year mortgages.
- Make a separate "principal only" payment in addition to any minimal monthly payment on credit cards and loans.
- Avoid making late payments because any subsequent payments will be applied to penalty charges or late fees, and the principal balance will not be decreased.
- Set a goal to repay any loan with interest as soon as possible.

Learning Points for Students and Parents

- Interest is an extra charge added to the principle balance or original loan amount.

- An individual's credit score will determine the amount of interest charged on a loan or extension of credit. The higher the credit score the lower the interest.
- Making minimum monthly payments on loans and credit cards will actually increase the amount of the outstanding debt.
- Minimum monthly payments are intentionally set-up to prolong the elimination of debts and increase profits to financial institutions.
- Extended loan repayment plans have created billions in additional revenue for credit card companies, financial institutions, and student loan companies.

CHAPTER 8

Credit Card Temptation

"The things we can't have, we want the most."
—Old Wive's Tale

What do all of the following items have in common? Chocolate, cheating on final exams, lying to your parents about your grades, a long kiss good night, smoking marijuana, or watching a wet T-shirt contest during spring break. They are all different forms of the same thing—temptation.

Since the beginning of time, people have been faced with temptation. Marketers use it to sell products and services to millions of consumers who are, for the most part, easily enticed by things they can't have.

Starting around the mid-1980s, credit card companies designed a new marketing strategy to attract what they termed as "new lifelong customers." Traditionally, if an individual wanted to apply for a credit card, he would have to meet certain income requirements and have an acceptable credit score. Based on the traditional guidelines, 99% of today's college students would not qualify because they have not established a credit history and do not have sufficient income at this stage of their lives.

After evaluating these two traditional guidelines, credit card companies designed a very ingenious plan to increase their customer base. They developed an application process specifically for students that almost guaranteed approval for every student applicant. Their only requirement for approval was that students be registered at a college or university. That's it. In short, if you are a registered college student, you're approved. This single move was very smart on behalf of credit card companies. It put them in a position to access five to six million potential new clients every academic year. These potential new clients are also known as high school students or college freshmen who cannot wait to get their first taste of freedom, often in the form of "plastic".

Every fall on college and university campuses nationwide, students are presented with one of the biggest temptations for young adults—a credit card application. Students are bombarded by credit card representatives with solicitations online, through e-mail, in college bookstores, and in person. It's all very alluring, attractive, and seductive. Each solicitation has in bold print, YOU ARE AUTOMATICALLY APPROVED. APPLY TODAY. The live representatives even offer free gifts such as T-shirts, music CDs, mini-radios, and school paraphernalia to each student who signs up for a new card. These companies have free reign on many of the largest campuses in the United States. Some colleges and universities even enter into financial agreements with credit card companies that pay schools millions of dollars annually for the rights to solicit current students as well as alumni. Today's credit card companies will create cards with the school name and mascot to make them more appealing to unsuspecting students, faculty and alumni.

Like any temptation, the thought of being able to buy the latest Jay-Z CD, a new pair of Jordans, or a new iPod is almost impossible for any college student to resist. Throw all that in with the ability to buy what they want when they want it, without any input from their parents. This makes a credit card seem like a necessity for college life.

Credit card companies rely on the fact that college students are young and carefree. They understand students better than the students understand themselves because they have done their research. These companies' main goal is to get their cards into as many wallets or purses as possible. The most disturbing part is that these students are eligible for multiple credit cards as well as department store cards. According to Nellie Mae, student loan guarantor, 76% of undergraduate students in 2005 had a credit card. In addition, Nellie Mae reported that 91% of students in their last year of college had at least one credit card.

In light of these patterns, it is not hard to understand how students slowly acquire more debt than they can afford, which is an oxymoron because many of these students do not have jobs and cannot afford to have any credit card debt.

College students need to know that credit cards can be great to have in times of need. Many will need one for certain transactions like car rentals, unexpected airline tickets home, or even to help pay for school-related supplies. It is very important that students develop a working understanding of the responsibility associated with credit card use. When students act responsibly, they can prevent negative financial situations that have the potential to follow them for many years after graduation.

Historically, people have learned how to use credit cards by making costly financial mistakes and errors. Many individuals continue to make the same mistakes throughout their lives because they either have limited knowledge of credit card use or inaccurate information. College students are at the beginning stages of their financial life. Developing an understanding of the proper use of credit cards is priceless.

The best remedy for any problem is prevention. Therefore, students must take the initiative to create a financially sound foundation during this period in their lives. The following steps will help students understand the importance of being responsible with credit card usage.

1. **Students should make sure they get their parents' permission before applying for credit cards.**
   College students really do not like this step because they want to feel independent in their decisions. Hopefully doing this will put some pressure on students to keep their parents informed about any credit applications or credit card use. Students who ask for their parents' approval before applying for credit cards are more likely to receive warnings and advice on this subject because many parents have made their own mistakes associated with credit cards. The students who chose to ignore this step may regret it the future.

2. **Do not apply for more than two credit cards.**
   Two cards are plenty for any college student. The more cards a student has, the more risk he has for creating more debt or creating a negative credit history. Students should use one for purchases and the other strictly for emergencies, which do not include one-day sales at the mall or front-row tickets for the latest concert. Students should also make sure that both of the cards are not at their limits at any given time. If both cards are at their limits, students may be tempted to apply for additional credit cards. Be smart and stick to two cards.

3. **Never use your credit card to purchase items for friends.**
The quickest way to end any friendship is to have a disagreement about money. Remember, your credit card is money, therefore, never purchase items for friends with the promise of being reimbursed when the bill arrives. Often when the bill arrives, friends get amnesia. Suddenly, you become the bad guy because you need their money in order to send in your payment. Once the purchased item has been used (e.g. clothes worn, tickets used, food eaten, etc.), there is very little incentive for them to pay you. The novelty has worn off for them, but *you* still owe the money. If you value your friendships, just say no to those who ask to use your credit cards.

4. **Credit card purchases are not free.**
Many students forget that the items they purchase with credit cards must be paid for with real money. When some students use credit cards to make purchases, they do not acknowledge they are actually spending money. At some point, cash must be exchanged for the items purchased. Students do not realize how much they have purchased on a credit card until the monthly bill arrives. The reason for this feeling is because up to this point in their lives they have always made purchases with cash or debit cards. Therefore, buying items on credit feels different because they get to keep their cash in their pocket during the purchase. This type of mind-set can get students into financial trouble. They may purchase more than they can afford to repay, which leads to late or missed payments. Buying items on credit can become addictive, and if students are not careful, they will be paying for an expensive credit education.

5. Develop the habit of paying bills on time every month. This is probably the most important of all the steps: *Pay your bills on time.* This point cannot be stressed enough. Students should pay off their entire balance for each card every month on time. If this habit is developed at an early age, it will help to establish a great credit history and solid financial foundation. Very few individuals are able to master the art of paying all of their bills on time. Thirty percent of a student's credit score is based on timeliness of bill payments. Also, they can avoid late fees, over-the-limit fees, and additional interest charges by paying bills on time. This life-long skill will be beneficial at any stage of life.

6. Learn to keep credit card temptations under control. College students must understand that they are the prime targets for credit card companies. Executives have spent countless hours coming up with ways to entice young consumers. They make their cards appear alluring by tempting students with all the things they can buy with that little piece of plastic. Even before students make it to their freshman English class they may have multiple opportunities to apply for a variety of credit cards. Having their very own credit cards is a temptation that could have life-long effects. Credit card usage can be a strong temptation, especially among students. It can be hard for students to resist when they are being bombarded with solicitations that credit card purchases are cool and hip. Students should understand that there is nothing cool or hip about credit card debt, bad credit, or limited employment opportunities. Temptations are strong, but hopefully, the desire to be financially responsible will be stronger among students.

Learning Points for Students and Parents

- All college students, especially freshmen, are the prime targets for credit card marketers.
- Students must resist the temptation to apply for credit cards. They should think about how credit card debt will impact their futures.
- Students should not accept free "stuff" from credit card marketers in exchange for several years of credit card debt. It is cheaper to buy a T-shirt, CD case or college cap with cash. Be smart.
- Parents should make sure to monitor students' intentions when they apply for credit cards, and they should monitor the amount of accumulated credit card debt.
- Parents should caution students on ways to avoid the temptation to acquire several credit cards during college.
- Parents need to monitor mail for any increase in credit card bills.

CHAPTER 9

Students Must Own It

"No one plans to be broke, it just happens."
—Unknown

Today's college students are at a pivotal point in the history of American economics. Historically, these students are earning significantly more income after college in comparison to their parents at the same age. Although these students are earning more, economic indicators reveal that the number of personal bankruptcies and home foreclosures are at an all-time high, while savings and investments are at an all-time low. These economic indicators clearly show that many college graduates as well as other individuals of their generation are still not in control of their finances.

Students are charged with the duty to become "fiscally fit" while in college. In addition to having enough academic credit hours to graduate, students must make sure they are taking the initiative to get educated about their personal finances.

The first rule of thumb for students is to know how much money or income they have available. If they are smart enough to understand complex math calculations, scientific theories, and journalistic formats, they should be able to master how to develop an effective budget, which is another lifelong skill that will assist students with managing money. Again, without a budget, students do not have a clue as to how much money they need to meet their monthly expenses. Money management is the first skill that students need to master in order to create a strong financial foundation.

DOLLARS AND SENSE

Students who do not know how to manage money are prime targets for impulse buying.

Younger students in their first two years of college tend to have one source of income—their parents. Students in this category have to know realistically how much money their parents are able to give them at any given time. Many parents are burdened with increased college costs in addition to their own financial obligations (e.g., home mortgage, car loans, insurance, etc.). Therefore, the amount of income available for their children attending college may be limited. Knowing that they have a limited amount of money coming in, these students must make sure they are cautious of the new debts they create. A harsh reality for millions of freshmen is that their parents' income is not limitless.

Many freshmen and sophomores are not in a position to have jobs because most are still adjusting to college life. Some parents will not allow their children to work during their first two years of school because of this adjustment. Due to their lack of knowledge related to money management, many young students run into financial trouble early in their college careers. Younger students are more prone to be more impulsive with their spending in comparison to older ones.

These students are new to the college experience and are more susceptible to unnecessary spending. Many freshmen and sophomores want to make sure they participate in all the college activities, which can become very costly. Pressured to make up for their limited available cash, many students will turn to credit cards to make sure they are not ostracized for missing out on events such as spring break vacations, the latest fashions, or college night life.

The greatest fear of any college freshman is to be left out. So if it is a money issue, they will use any resources available to ensure they are part of the in crowd. These early college years are peer pressure on steroids. If students have not been exposed to good money management skills by their parents, they are at risk for developing poor habits related to handling money.

Some students may get part-time jobs during their junior year. They may start to live off campus, acquire cars, and begin to gain more independence from their parents. There may also be a decline in the financial support available by some parents who are unable to continue sending money as students advance through college. These students actually have to seek jobs to help offset their college costs. Managing money at this stage becomes extremely important because these students have certain obligations they must meet (e.g., rent, food, tuition, books, and clothes).

Typically, this is the time when students establish their first checking or savings accounts. Although students are not really focused on savings, establishing various accounts marks the beginning of their financial responsibility. Students learn quickly that if they do not manage their money well, they are at risk for increased fees related to bounced checks, also known as insufficient funds.

DOLLARS AND SENSE

80% of high school seniors have opened bank accounts, and more than a quarter have bounced a check.

—*Time* magazine/Jumpstart Coalition

It is not unusual for college students to bounce several checks when they open their first checking account. This occurs because students have not been taught how to balance a checkbook. Students deposit money in the bank and spend it without any tracking system in place. Balancing a checkbook is a new life skill for students that will take them time to develop like good study habits. Unfortunately, learning this skill can be costly if it takes them too long to understand the process. The last thing any college student is thinking about during homecoming weekend is balancing a checkbook.

How to Balance a Checkbook

1. Start with ending balance from previous month's bank statement.
2. Add all current deposits made to checking account, including direct deposits, ATM and teller deposits and any interest generated by the account.
3. Subtract all current withdrawals from checking account, including ATM usage, foreign ATM fees, electronic funds transfers (e.g., online payments or purchases), teller withdrawals and any monthly banking fees.
4. Ending balance: Amount of money remaining in banking account after the addition of deposits (credits) and subtraction of withdrawals (debit).

Although the above steps are very effective, they really do not take into account the new variable in balancing a checkbook, debit or check card use. Students not only are novices in the use of checks, they also are using the debit card to make purchases at a variety of retailers. Many people, not just students, are not consistent in recording all of their debit card transactions in their checking account ledger. Debit cards are rapidly replacing the use of cash in routine purchases of food, clothing, and entertainment.

When students fail to consistently record debit card transactions they increase the likelihood of overdrawing their account.

An effective strategy to monitor checking account balances is to use online banking services. Students can record all their checks in their checking account ledger and monitor debit card transactions online. Ease of use with online banking will allow students to monitor their accounts as often as they would like. As checks clear their checking account and their available balance is decreased students have to be mature enough to stop making purchases using their debit card due to the limited money available in their account.

Failing to closely monitor their checking account, including outstanding checks and debit card transactions, will result in bounced checks and increased bank charges. Insufficient fund fees (NSF fees) are charged to checking accounts when there is not enough money in the account to cover the payment of a check. These fees usually range from $24.99 to $39.99 and can be charged for each check or debit card transaction that does not clear a checking account due to lack of funds (money).

It is recommended that students monitor their checking accounts at least every forty-eight hours to verify if outstanding checks cleared the account and more importantly, verify how much money is available.

According to a recent commercial, Bank of America processes over forty million checks every day. What if just 3% of these checks bounced at a rate of $30 per check. They would generate *$36 million every day* in additional revenue. That is $1.08 billion per month or $13 billion per year from bounced checks.

The following statement regarding bounced checks was made by a local branch manager at a bank located in Atlanta: *"I have been a banker for a national banking company for a number of years. Every day I am amazed at the number of people who overdraw their accounts on a daily basis. Each branch is responsible for pulling their daily overdraft list. The list tells us how many people have overdrawn their accounts and how many overdrafts they have. The number of clients on the report can vary each day depending on the size of the branch. You can have anywhere from one to fifty clients a day on the report."*

"It is our responsibility to contact the people on the overdraft list to make sure they have not lost or had their debit or checkbook stolen. I am always appalled at the number of people I speak with who are not concerned that they just gave the bank $128 for multiple bounced checks. Most of the customers with repeated NSF fees can be linked to inaccurate recording of their transactions. They are relying too much on the computer (the bank) to keep records for them."

"The advice I would give parents and students is to make sure they keep an accurate record of their transactions to prevent any charges related to bounced checks."

In addition to eventually being forced to learn how to balance their checkbooks, students must learn how to make deposits, cash payroll checks, and write personal checks to pay bills. These are lifelong money management skills. Students who fail to establish these skills will have recurring financial problems throughout their adult lives.

Students who are in their last year of college or those having entered graduate school have even larger financial responsibilities in comparison to their younger counterparts. These students are typically totally responsible for their financial decisions, including credit card acquisition and use. The average amount of debt for students graduating from college is $19,202, according to the November 2005 issue of *Careers and Colleges* magazine. The keyword is *average.*

Since students around this age are more independent for the most part, they also tend to use credit cards to help offset the cost of tuition and living expenses. Students are currently facing higher tuition costs and increased student loan debt, and many are using credit cards to actually finish college.

The Good Ole Days

While in college I had four roommates, and we shared a house in Washington, D.C. We moved in right before I started my junior year at Howard University. Since we rented a house, we were responsible for the utilities in addition to the rent. One of my roommates, Tim, had recently graduated from college and was working as a pharmacist. My other roommates, Rory, Jimmy, and Joe were also entering their junior year. Some of us had limited or no financial support from our parents, but all of us had part-time or full-time jobs. Only one of my roommates did not need to have a job—he was on a full academic scholarship.

DOLLARS AND SENSE

Students who maintain good grades in high school and college may never have to work during college.

Although most of us had jobs and access to our own money, rarely did any of our bills get paid on time. It was not unusual to come home from class and discover the heat had been turned off or the telephone had been disconnected. This was not as much of a problem during the summer months, but the winters in Washington, D.C., are very cold, especially when there is no heat. Our phone was placed in various names due to non-payment of large past due bills stemming from long-distance calls. Our landlord owned and operated a store next door to our house, but that still did not prompt us to pay our rent on time.

These patterns of slow payment or non-payments lasted my junior and senior years. In addition to irregular payments on utility bills, we also paid credit card bills sporadically. These infrequent payments had a direct impact on each of our financial futures.

Years after we had all graduated from college and started our professional careers, one thing remained—all those unpaid credit card debts. If we had better managed our money over the years, we could have totally erased all of our debts, including most of our student loans. My roommates and I, like most college students, made several bad financial decisions because we had never been exposed to sound financial strategies at an early age.

The core of good money management skills is to know how much money you have coming in monthly (income) and how much you have going out (expenses). This means that students must take time to figure out exactly how much income they have in relation to their monthly expenses. Using this advice, we should have written down a budget similar to the following while we were still in college.

Account	Monthly Payment	Due Date
Rent	$275	1/1/2007
Phone	$50	1/15/2007
Heating Oil	$25	1/1/2007
Electric	$20	1/15/2007
Best Buy	$15	1/25/2007
Visa	$20	1/20/2007
Macy's	$20	1/20/2007
TOTAL*	**$425**	

Income	
Payroll	$750
Parents	$300
TOTAL	**$1,050**

**Chart does not include food or tuition costs.*

It is critical for a student's financial survival to know the exact amount of his monthly expenses. This information will let him assess where he is financially and alert him to any impending dangers. Not knowing this information is like walking into a financial ambush. To confirm this fact, consider the financial situation of the average American.

Land of the Free

Americans' savings percentage has declined to an historical low of -1.0% for 2006, according to a report released by the Department of Commerce. It says that if a person has an annual salary of $30,000, he will spend $30,300. This is the lowest savings rate among Americans since The Great Depression. These facts indicate that the average American continues to charge items he really cannot afford.

DOLLARS AND SENSE

In preparation for the 2007 Super Bowl, 2.5 million Americans purchased HDTVs and another 1.3 million purchased furniture including home entertainment centers just for the game. —National Retail Federation

There are more than nine hundred million credit and debit cards in circulation in the United States, but there are only about three hundred million people living in the country. This means that on average there are at least three credit or debit cards for each man, woman, and child. It is very clear that individuals with high credit card debt and low savings accounts correlate to problems managing money. These types of indicators reveal that millions of Americans have not developed good money management skills.

Millions of college students don't plan to be broke after graduation. The reality is that many of them will become financially challenged because they have not developed effective methods of handling their money. In order to change this trend, students must start by learning the basics of good money management, which includes balancing a checkbook and organizing expenses. This is the foundation for establishing lifelong money management empowerment. Without these skills, students will continue to have financial problems.

The Bill Payment System

One of the most important aspects of establishing money management skills and creditworthiness is directly related to paying accounts on time. Consistently re-paying financial obligations is an excellent way for students to establish themselves financially, and it will help to increase their credit scores. Late payments create serious financial consequences for students, especially with a new provision that is being utilized by credit card companies to create billions at the expense of unsuspecting consumers-*universal default.*

Whenever a customer makes a late payment on any open account (e.g., home loan, auto loan, credit card, student loan,etc.), credit card companies have a clause in their contract that allows them to increase their interest rates to the maximum allowed amount. Universal default can occur with just one missed or late payment on any account. These increased interest rates can be applied to all of the consumer's credit card accounts, even if they have never made a late payment to the credit issuer.

In an effort to combat universal default, students need a strategy that will ensure all of their bills will be paid on time. The bill payment system (BPS) is a proven system that will help students prevent any late or missed payments. BPS consists of the following steps:

1. Obtain a desktop calendar.
2. Create a list of all monthly bills, including due dates.
3. Write each bill on the calendar according to the corresponding due date (e.g., rent/mortgage will be written on the first, auto loan will be written on the fifteenth, student loan on

the eighth,etc.). Continue to write each bill on the calendar until all of them have been entered for the month.

4. Write the entire list of bills at the bottom of the page below the calendar entries for a given month and include the total amount of their recorded expenses at the bottom of the calendar for each month of the year.
5. Write the dates income is received. If you have a job, enter the word *payroll* on the dates you receive your check (e.g. weekly, bi-weekly, monthly or on a certain date). If a student does not work he would record the date he receives or expects to receive income from other sources such as parents, student aid or student stipend. Students would list the total amount of income at the bottom of the calendar for each month of the year.
6. Follow steps 1 through 4 to complete each month of the calendar, January through December. Add the total monthly expenses for each month and record the projected annual amount on the last page of the calendar. The same process can be done for monthly income. Once all of the entries have been entered for each month, this part of the process is complete.

The theory behind the bill payment system is that students will have a written guide to assist them in knowing exactly when each of their monthly bills is due. The repetitious use of the calendar to make payments will help students develop a sensitivity to the due dates. Usually after using this system for about two months, students start to correlate certain dates of the month with the corresponding bill due dates. The due dates will gain significance similar to other important dates in their lives. This may sound trivial, but keep in mind the financial and personal consequences that can be attributed to late or missed payments.

November 2007

Sun	Mon	Tue	Wed	Thu	Fri	Sat
			1 Mortgage—$1069 Rent—$329	*2*	*3* Payday	*4* Gas—$100
5	*6*	*7* Home Ins.—$60 Target-Visa—$50	*8* Auto Ins.—$160 Trash—$20	*9* Electric—$112	*10*	*11*
12	*13*	*14* Capital One—$75	*15* Auto Loan—$493 Phone—$115	*16* Student Loan—$255 Student Loan—$155	*17* Payday	*18* Banana Republic—$25
19 Best Buy—$254	*20*	*21* Cell Phone—$200	*22*	*23*	*24*	*25*
26	*27*	*28*	*29* Water—$50 Alarm—$15 The GAP—$25	*30*		

Mortgage	Auto Insurance	Phone	Cell Phone
Rent	Trash	Student Loan	Water
Gas	Electric	Student Loan	Alarm
Home Insurance	Capital One	Banana Rep.	Nordstrom
Target Visa	Auto Loan	Best Buy	

Each month as a bill is paid, students will be able to cross it off the corresponding date. In addition to crossing off paid bills by date, students will also be able to keep track of paid bills by crossing them off the list at the bottom of the calendar each month.

The bill paying system will work equally as well using modern technology such as a PDA with reminders, computer desktop calendars, Quicken software, or automated payments set up through online banking services with the free bill pay feature. Either method can be effective in avoiding late payments, but it is recommended that students start with the manual method until they get comfortable with implementing the process monthly.

This system will not only prevent students from being exposed to universal default guidelines, it also will save them money by preventing late fees, over-the-limit fees, and bounced checks. This is a proven system that can be utilized by students and their parents, if needed. In order for this system to work effectively students must monitor their calendars at least weekly.

Many people have no system in making their monthly bill payments. Therefore, students who master this system will have better control of their finances, in addition to peace of mind, knowing all of their bills have been paid on time.

Learning Points for Students and Parents

- The 2006 savings rate in the U.S. was -1.0%. This means Americans are spending more than the income they earn. Example: Annual income is $40,000, annual spending is $40,400.
- Money management is a very important skill for students to learn and master.
- Money from parents is the primary income source for most freshmen and sophomore college students.
- Due to lack of knowledge related to money management, college students are prone to increased bounced checks.
- The banking industry makes billions of dollars annually from fees related to bounced checks.
- Students must learn how to balance a checkbook.
- The BPS (billing payment system) will help students and parents keep their bills organized. It will also help them make monthly payments on time.
- Pay all bills in full and on time every month.

CHAPTER 10

Financial Influence of Parents

"Do as I say, not as I do."
—Hattie K. Thomas, concerned parent

The headline of a national newspaper read, GOOD EDUCATION, GOOD JOB, BAD CREDIT. The article told a story that is common among today's college graduates. It featured a young lady who was an alumnus of a prominent women's liberal arts college. She had a good education and a good job making $60,000 a year, but that is where the real story began. In spite of graduating from one of the nation's top schools and securing a well-paying consulting job, she still had a big problem. While in college, she accumulated $70,000 worth of debt.

These debts included credit cards, an auto loan, and student loans. Late, slow, and missed payments caused her credit rating to plummet. Reality set in after graduation when she had difficulty establishing utility service in her new apartment. She stated in the article that because of her bad credit she had to leave hefty deposits in order to have her services connected.

This was her first real lesson on how important it is to establish a good credit history during college. In the article, she explained that she started to educate herself about personal finance by reading books because her parents did not give her a good background on the subject of personal finance.

Take a minute to understand the magnitude of this situation, which is being played out across college campuses nationwide. Parents have enough knowledge to make sure their children can read, write, and comprehend an array of subjects from world history to calculus, but many of them do not have the information to help prevent their children from getting into financial trouble.

Parents make sure that their children have help with things like the SAT, ACT, high school exit exams, college entrance exams, and financial aid paperwork. They expend a lot of energy stressing the importance of good grades in school, but give little thought that their children are flunking the one subject that every person needs to master—personal finance.

Many parents do not understand the impact they have on their children's financial decisions. When they do not have a good understanding of personal finance (e.g., income, debt, credit, investing, etc.), they tend to pass on bad financial habits to their children. It is virtually impossible for parents to teach their children about personal finance without having adequate knowledge on this subject.

Most students receive very little education and guidance regarding personal finance from their parents, teachers, and other faculty members. High school students have limited exposure to topics like money management, creditworthiness, debt management, or wealth accumulation techniques. Due to the increased financial consequences facing today's college students, it is very important that parents ensure that their children have early exposure to topics related to personal finance.

DOLLARS AND SENSE

Less than 30% of young Americans take at least one week of course work related to personal finance during high school.

—Jump$tart

This education should be established or initiated as early as possible, but at the latest by high school. These students have the intellect to understand the basic concepts of personal finance and their education on this topic is imperative. Students leaving high school and entering college will encounter many choices related to personal finance. If parents have not ensured that their children are prepared for this transition, it could prove to be costly for both the student and their parents.

DOLLARS AND SENSE

If a high school student can not manage $1,000 received from his summer job, how will he be prepared to manage $40,000 when he gets his first real job?

Knowledge related to personal finance can have a generational impact on today's parents and students. History is a very good indicator of this theory. Families who understand the fundamental concepts of personal finance not only pass this information on to their offspring, but they also practice these concepts in their everyday lives. Wealthy families tend to pass on information, verbally and non-verbally (actions), that assists their children with preserving as well as creating additional wealth.

In contrast, many middle or lower income families tend to show their children how to handle finances from a mind-set of scarcity. Students develop skills such as money or credit management by watching their parents deal with a lack of money or issues related to having negative credit. When children are exposed to certain positive financial beliefs related to credit, savings, investing, and budgeting, they are more likely to adopt these habits and utilize them as they mature into adults. The same is true when children are exposed to the opposite, such as arguments about the lack of money, disconnected utility services, repossessions, or foreclosures.

This is not to imply that middle- and lower-class families do not teach their children any valuable skills related to personal finance. The reality is that parents who have experienced financial success have a certain level of knowledge that can be passed on to their children. Socioeconomic status is not important. What is important is the possession of knowledge on how to achieve financial success using personal finance.

If this line of reasoning is not valid, why are millions of Americans intrigued with Donald Trump's reality show *The Apprentice*? Viewers tune in to get advice on how to make money from one of the richest men in America. Just think about the lessons related to personal finance that "The Donald" will pass on to his children.

A great example of this theory is evidenced by researching wealthy families like the Rockefellers, Kennedys, and Duponts. The matriarchs and patriarchs of these families created enormous amounts of wealth during their lifetimes. Although this wealth was originally created in some cases fifty, sixty or even a hundred years ago, their families have been able to maintain and expand it. The reason these families remain wealthy is due to financial concepts, guidelines, and rules that were created by their ancestors that have been passed down from generation to generation, therefore the wealth will continue to grow for many years to come.

In contrast to wealthy families, there are millions of families who have not been exposed to sound financial strategies or who have limited knowledge about topics like credit, stocks, savings, entrepreneurship, real estate investing, and mutual funds. Many Americans have had little or no education related to effective personal finance guidelines. When individuals are not exposed to these concepts and wealth-producing principles, they tend to create their own rules related to personal finance.

Parents that create their own rules such as paying bills late, making impulsive purchases, compromising their credit and accumulating high levels of debt, indirectly teach their children poor personal financial principles. If parents are ineffective money managers, there is a strong probability that these same inadequate skills may be passed on to their children. Parents must keep in mind that their actions, especially those related to personal finance, have a stronger influence on their children in comparison to just talking about it.

This is what young people mean when they say, "Don't talk about it, be about it."

Parents must understand that teaching their children about good personal finance is no different than teaching them good table manners or good hygiene. Parents need to ensure that their children are sent out into the world with effective knowledge regarding the importance of checking accounts, personal credit, money management, and real estate investing.

Unfortunately, too many parents are not equipped to pass this type of information on to the next generation. Consumer debt is at record levels, personal bankruptcies and home foreclosures are rising nationwide and people are saving less than 1% of their income. There is also a nationwide increase in the number of "payday" loan companies that specialize in high-interest short-term loans for low to moderate income families.

DOLLARS AND SENSE

Between 25 million and 56 million adults are un-banked (e.g. not using mainstreem insured institutions.)

—*The Vineyard News*

Such trends illustrate the huge void related to financial education. As this knowledge gap is likely to continue, today's college students may not gain the knowledge needed to prepare their own children on how to handle their personal finances.

Think about this fact: 3% of the people in the United States control 90% of the wealth. According to recent census results, there are three hundred million people in the United States. Based on these figures, nine million out of three hundred million control the vast majority of the wealth in this country.

Parents must make a commitment not only to learn about personal finance, but to develop a new financially responsible mindset. This increase in financial literacy among parents will afford them the ability to give students sound advice on personal finance. This will also help to alleviate generational financial illiteracy among high school and college students. Every parent's dream is for his child to have the best opportunities in life. If this feeling still holds true, parents must gain the knowledge that will enable them to advise students about financial decisions that have life-changing implications.

Steps to Help Parents Educate Their Children About Personal Finance:

1. Educate yourself by reading, researching, and taking courses related to personal finance.
2. Teach students the difference between income and expenses.
3. Stress the importance of delayed gratification.
4. Instruct students on how to set up a financial budget.
5. Subscribe to personal finance and business publications(e. g., *The Wall Street Journal, Black Enterprise* magazine, *Kiplinger* magazine, *Money* magazine, *Fortune* magazine and *Forbes* magazine).
6. Discuss various topics related to personal finance with students including credit, savings, and money management.

7. Understand the importance of developing a positive financial mind-set.
8. Stress the importance of establishing and maintaining satisfactory credit at an early age.
9. Encourage students to get educated on personal finance before entering college.
10. Develop the skills to make sure students have their personal finances in order, and show them rather than tell them what to do.

CHAPTER 11

Learn the Game

"The quality of your living depends entirely on your ability to play the game, and I play the game ..."

—Intro. *The Documentary*
by The Game, rap artist

In 1997 Tiger Woods won his first Masters tournament at the age of twenty-one. Four years later in 2001, he won his second Masters tournament title. The very next year, Tiger won his third Masters tournament. He was only twenty-six years old. Three years later, after a one-hole playoff with Chris Dimarco, Tiger Woods sank a fifteen-foot putt to become the youngest player in Masters' history to win at least four tournaments. He accomplished this record earlier than Jack Nicklaus who won his fourth tournament at the age of thirty-two and Arnold Palmer who won his fourth title at the age of thirty-four.

Players, writers, and fans alike felt that Tiger's fourth Masters' win was nothing short of a miracle.

It is safe to say that Tiger Woods undoubtedly knows how to play the game of golf. It has been widely speculated that Tiger Woods has been playing since the age of three. Tiger's image is internationally known for his passion and relentless commitment to excellence. After his most recent win in August 2006, Tiger regained the number one ranking in the world among golf professionals.

If a high school student told you that he was capable of beating Tiger Woods in a round of golf, what would you think? Here is the catch, this student has never played organized golf before, but he has no doubt that he can beat Tiger Woods on any given day.

You would probably think, *This kid must be crazy, delusional—or both.* What is the likelihood that any student with no prior golfing experience would be able to beat the world's greatest golfer?

The reason this proposition sounds so unrealistic is because our rational mind tells us that if professional golfers have difficulty beating Tiger, there is no way an inexperienced high school student can defeat him.

The same holds true for personal finance. How can we expect high school and college students or their parents to compete with large financial institutions with regards to money and credit?

In the game of personal finance, students and their parents need to understand they are competing against an opponent who actually developed the game. Any time a player is competing against an opponent who created the rules of a game, it is nearly impossible to achieve a victory without thorough knowledge.

DOLLARS AND SENSE

Tiger Woods has been playing golf for at least twenty-six years. Banks, credit card companies, and other financial institutions have been playing the game of finance for the last one hundred-fifty years.

The best example of this theory is the way gamblers compete at casinos. Every gambler—professional and novice—has the feeling that he can beat the house. Unfortunately, this rarely occurs because casinos set the rules on who wins and who loses. This is affectionately known as "house rules." In this same regard, banks, credit card companies, and financial institutions have a set of rules that ensure they will make profits 99.9% of the time.

College students enter the personal finance game every semester when they apply for credit cards or open a bank account. However, most do not realize that a game is being played until they are thousands of dollars in debt, usually well after graduation.

Remember, the quality of your living depends entirely on your ability to play the game. This statement sums it up very nicely. If high school and college students plan to compete in the game of personal finance, then their first step is to learn how to compete. The vast majority of students enrolled on campuses nationwide have limited knowledge about the credit or personal finance game.

Banks, credit card companies, and financial institutions rely on the fact that America's best and brightest have not been educated on personal finance. This gives the institutions an unfair advantage, ensuring that they will benefit financially throughout a student's lifetime. College students must make a commitment to spend some time learning how to keep score when it comes to their personal finances. Although there are thousands of college majors, there is arguably only one field of study that students will use forever—personal finance.

This game, like all others, has winners and losers. The people who continually lose do not realize they are doing so. Students will have to become aware of the rules of the game and take time to practice these rules.

Bishop Dale C. Bronner, pastor of Word of Faith Family Worship Cathedral in Atlanta, Georgia, said it best in one of his sermons: "*Practice does not make perfect, practice makes you better.*" Students need to start practicing their skills at an early age. Practice in this area increases one's chance of having a bright financial future, as students will learn what is out of bounds, how to keep score, and know the difference between offense and defense.

Here are some of the ground rules for students who want to champion the game of personal finance:

1. Learn the rules. Make a committed effort to learn about credit cards, student loans, bank accounts (checking and savings), money management, savings, interest, fees, revolving debt, investments,etc. All of these areas work together, and it is important to know how one affects another. Having knowledge of one area without understanding another is synonymous to a golfer knowing how to make a putt, but not knowing how to tee off, make a chip shot, or read the greens.
2. Research all areas of personal finance. One of the best sources of research is the Internet. Some great sites to explore are www.mycollegefinance.com, www.bankrate.com, www.myfico.com, www.cardweb.com, www.americanexpressfinance.com and www.equifax.com. In addition to using websites, it is a great idea to subscribe to magazines and newspapers that focus on personal finance. Some great examples of these are *The Wall Street Journal, Black Enterprise* magazine, *Kiplinger Personal Finance, Fortune* magazine, *Money* magazine, your local newspaper's business section, or the personal finance sections of *Fortune, Forbes,* or *Barron's.* Books also are a great source of information. (See Suggested Reading in Appendix B.) Start with your school or local library and bookstores.
3. Get organized. Students must develop the habit of getting all of their personal finances organized. When bills, bank statements, credit card payments, etc., are not in order, students and parents are at a distinct disadvantage. Financial institutions make the bulk of their money in late fees,

penalties, and interest/finance charges. Consumers who do not develop a system to keep their finances in order will pay more in these additional fees. The bottom line is to develop the habit of being organized. Many companies plan to make increased revenues from your disorganization every month.

4. Practice, practice, practice. It is rumored that Tiger Woods hits a thousand golf balls every day—rain or shine. This daily goal was highlighted on a recent commercial from his corporate sponsor, American Express. The commercial gives a list of things Tiger could do on a rainy day, implying he could take it easy due to the rain. Tiger's reply: "*There are no rainy days,*" meaning he is relentless in his pursuit of excellence. Students must adopt a similar mind-set to be relentless in practicing the rules of personal finance daily. They cannot practice sporadically. Instead, their preparation must be like they were expecting to challenge a professional competitor such as a bank or credit card company. Students need to realize that their competition: banks, credit card companies and financial institutions are playing this game every hour of every day. Their goal is to make profits daily, not every now and then.
5. Start keeping score. Consumers fall into two categories: those who pay interest on their debt and those who make interest on their investments. Students should learn how much interest they are paying on credit cards, student loans, and other financial items. Once they know the amount of interest, they can develop a plan to decrease or eliminate it from their finances. In addition to interest, students must keep track of the amount of monthly and annual debt they are accumulating while they are in school. This is very important because it is the first step to gaining control of your finances. Students should also be

> aware of how much they are paying to banks in late, over-the-limit fees, and fees for insufficient funds. If students do not know these things, they will not know the score of the game.

There are three types of students: those who are watching the game, those who don't know that there is a game, and those who are playing the game. Into which category do you fit?

Some students know the rules to the game, which is evident when they invest their money, purchase real estate, start college businesses, and rent/lease housing to others. These students have been exposed to the game from their parents, family members, or other personal finance mentors. Students who learn the rules to the game at an early age will be in a position to benefit for the rest of their lives. You must decide whether you want to compete like a professional or be one of the millions of spectators watching from the comfort of the sidelines.

CHAPTER 12

Debt at the Speed of Light

"It is easy to take over
from those who have not thought ahead."
—Sun Tzu, *The Art of War*

Credit card debt in America is at historical levels, but credit card companies are still not content. While most people are trying to find ways to curb their debt and get control of their finances, credit card companies are planning new and improved ways to increase their revenue. They have developed new technology that will enable users to make purchases even faster.

This new technology is known as *Blink*. Credit cards come with an implanted chip that allows the user to wave or tap the card in front of a special terminal to complete purchases, which will take less time because consumers will not have to give their card to potential merchants. Since the credit card never exchanges hands, it is estimated that this change will take twenty seconds off the average time it takes to make a typical credit card purchase.

Before you are ready to *Blink*, let's review a few facts:

- The average college student owes almost $3,800 in credit card debts in addition to their student loans.
- Americans bought more than $2 trillion worth of "stuff" on credit in 2006.
- Current outstanding debt on credit cards—the "revolving" part that Americans don't pay off every month—totals nearly $700 billion, up from $50 billion in 1980.
- Three out of five American families cannot pay off their credit cards each month. Their running annual balances average about $8,400 per household.
- Americans paid more than $24 billion in credit card fees in 2004.
- According to www.debtclock.com, debt in America is at $7 trillion.

Based on the above facts, why do credit card companies feel that consumers, including high school and college students, need the ability to make faster purchases?

JP Morgan-Chase is one of the nation's largest credit card issuers with more than ninety million credit cards in circulation. If each of these users charge at least $20 on their new card with Blink technology—you know consumers have to test it to see if it really works—that will be $1.8 billion in new charges. If that sounds like a lot, take into consideration that the average credit card transaction is about $82. Imagine how much that would be in new charges—about $7.38 billion. Throw in some late fees, over-the-limit fees, and finance charges, and $7.38 billion could easily increase to well over $10 billion in revenue in a short period of time.

Credit card companies have recently launched a huge

campaign to get consumers to increase their use of credit cards for purchases instead of using cash. A recent Visa commercial depicts a deli where everyone is singing, dancing and everything is flowing smoothly as long as customers are using credit cards to check out. One customer pulls out cash to pay for his purchase and everything in the commercial turns into chaos. The commercial gives a subliminal message that there is a problem when paying with cash instead of credit cards. Currently consumers use their credit cards fifty million times a day or six hundred times a second, but banks and credit companies want consumers to use them even more. These companies are betting that this new Blink technology will be the thing that will help increase consumer spending habits.

The convenience of credit and debit card use has increased dramatically. The most recent expansion of credit card acceptance has been seen at nationwide fast food chains and convenience stores like McDonald's and 7-Eleven. College students and consumers in general must be aware of the seduction of credit use and not be in such a hurry to accumulate debt.

Although many students are responsible with credit, a growing number are being severely affected by credit card debt. Recent studies from the Georgetown Credit Research Center indicate that 87.9% of all college students with credit cards pay their bills on time. The study also pointed out college students had smaller amounts of credit debt in comparison to older users. However, it is estimated that about 12% of college students with credit cards have payments at least thirty days past due. In comparison to older users, college students are nearly three times more likely to have seriously delinquent accounts—more than sixty days past due.

The latest figures from the 2005 Nellie Mae Credit Card usage study indicated that 76% of undergraduates had at least one credit card. There are an estimated sixteen million students enrolled in colleges and universities nationwide. Therefore, about twelve million college students have at least one credit card. Based on the above data from the Georgetown Credit Research Center, an estimated 1.5 million college students could have late or delinquent payments. This is a significant number of students who could be affected, not only by past-due bills, but with potentially bad credit. These figures are reported annually, which imply each school year there could be at least 1.5 million students who could be late or delinquent with their credit card payments. Although 1.5 million may not seem like a large number of affected students, keep in mind data from research may not be totally accurate—there might be more young adults with delinquent payments than what has been reported.

Credit card companies like to emphasize that "overall, college students are responsible with their credit card usage." These companies disregard the fact that every year more and more students are getting deeper into credit card debt at even younger ages. College students must understand that credit card companies are in the business of making money, period. It is in the credit card company's best interests to only publicize the positive aspects of usage among students. The reality is that students who repeatedly pay their bills late will subsequently create negative credit histories that put them at financial risk. Any negative reporting on a student's credit profile may have a noticeable impact on his academic and financial future as well as his employment options.

In Case of Emergency, Break Glass

For the students and parents reading this book who are saying, "Too late, I'm already deep in debt," the following steps will help you to eliminate your overall debt. These steps are not to be seen as a cookie cutter approach to eliminating debt. The degree of success in eliminating debt is always based on a student's drive, persistence and commitment.

1. **Make a decision that debt needs to be eliminated.** A sincere decision must be made that students or their

parents, want or need to reduce their debt.

2. **Create a budget.** This is probably the most important step in this process. Creating a budget will help to establish financial guidelines that must be followed to eliminate debt.
3. **Determine amount of debt.** All outstanding debts, including student loans and credit card debt should be totaled. This will serve as a starting point for eliminating debt.
4. **Develop a strategy.** There are a variety of debt-elimination theories. One is to pay off bills based on the interest rates. Debts with the highest interest rates are paid off first, then the next highest interest debt is paid until all debts are completely eliminated.

   Another theory is known as the Confidence Builder. This strategy is to pay off the smallest debts first, then continue this process until all debts are eliminated. This helps to build the confidence of the individual eliminating the debt because there is a sense of accomplishment (similar to a dieter seeing reduced weight on a scale). The increased confidence help motivate individuals to continue the debt-elimination process.

   The last debt reduction theory is known as S*tacking.* In this process, all debts are listed and prioritized based on which one should be paid first. The priority can be based on the account balances, interest rates or other criteria set by the individual. After the first debt is paid off, the amount that was being paid on the first bill is added to the payment of the second debt. For example, there is a monthly Visa monthly bill payment of $100. Once it is paid off the $100 would be added to the monthly bill for MasterCard. Now the total monthly amount paid on the MasterCard bill is $200 ($100 from the monthly Visa bill plus the $100 from the current MasterCard monthly bill). Once the second bill is paid off, the money from the first and second bill is added to the third bill. This process continues to add or *stack* payments, which helps to increase the rate of debt elimination.

5. **Stop creating any new debts**. Students and parents have to stop digging or creating new debts if they want to eliminate old ones. When new debts continue to be established, any progress is sabotaged.
6. **Be focused and disciplined.** Eliminating debt can take several months or years to complete. During this process students and parents must remain focused on reducing debt. Discipline is also needed to remain mentally strong.
7. **Manage Income.** To decrease the amount of overall debt, it is important to manage any current income. In order to reduce or eliminate debts, students and parents may need to generate additional income (full or part-time jobs) that can be applied to debts.
8. **Evaluate.** Evaluation of your debt- elimination program is needed monthly, quarterly and yearly. Knowing if debts are decreasing or if additional ones have been created will allow students and parents to alter their strategies.

Consumers nationwide are drowning in debt, yet credit card companies are allowed to use a variety of tactics to increase consumers' debt. Card companies have invested billions in *Blink* technology with the hopes of rapidly increasing their bottom line. The best defense is to plan out all credit card purchases, regardless of how fast you can make them. The real issue is not how fast you can buy the item, but rather how fast you can repay the debt. Students, please take your time. There's no rush to increase your credit card debt.

CHAPTER 13

What's the Score?

"If winning isn't everything, why do we keep score?"
—Vince Lombardi, Hall of Fame football coach

At the end of any competition, the only thing that matters is the final score. In sports, business, as well as the world of personal finance, everyone wants to be a winner. Children learn at a very early age that if you have the best score, you are rewarded and known as a winner among your peers. People have been in competition since the beginning of time, but without a score to measure the actual outcome of the event, any competition is meaningless.

Without scores, there would not be any close games, no come-from-behind victories, or the makings of a dynasty. The score is what gives meaning to historical comebacks. In 2004, the Boston Red Sox became the World Series Champions after being down three games to none to the New York Yankees in a best of seven League Championship series.

In addition to team accomplishments, there have been extraordinary individual performances like Kobe Bryant scoring eighty-one points against the Toronto Raptors during the 2005–2006 NBA season. No matter where a person goes in the world, and no matter what rules are used for the competition, the one thing that is universally important is the score.

DOLLARS AND SENSE

Remember, in life the only thing that separates the winners from the losers is the score.

When students enter college, they have a good understanding of the importance of good scores. They enter institutions of higher learning with many different goals in mind. They may want to produce good grades, attain various degrees, attend graduate school, and move into their chosen careers. If you ask any student what is considered a good SAT score, ACT score, or GMAT score, most will rattle off the answer without much thought. But if you ask them what is considered a good credit score, many will not be able to respond.

Good SAT or ACT scores are nice to have, but they have limited usefulness in life after college. Whatever test scores students achieve has already been utilized to assist them in getting into college. On the other hand, their credit scores are far more important, but students often do not realize this until well after their college days are over.

After graduation, college students often look forward to high-paying jobs, nice cars, great apartments, and the newest fashions. These will remain a dream if they have developed bad credit scores.

If a student does not have an "acceptable" credit score, companies may not make an employment offer. This means that even if a student has a great GPA, graduates summa cum laude, and has had great internships, his credit score could ultimately determine his employment opportunities.

Employers feel that if a student cannot manage his credit, he may be an increased risk in regards to job performance such as being punctual, trustworthy, or responsible. Potential employers have even indicated that people with bad credit are more likely to have increased absences, poor job performance, and questionable integrity. While students, parents, and faculty are promoting good grades and high SAT scores, students also must establish good credit scores to have the best options after college.

DOLLARS AND SENSE

A recent news story reported that several active duty military personnel were denied clearance to serve overseas due to bad credit. The military viewed these individuals as security risk and easy targets for bribes due to their credit/financial status.

Credit scores can range from 300–850. It is generally accepted that any score below 600 is bad credit. Average credit starts around 650, with good credit starting around 700. An excellent credit score is 750 and above, with 850 being supreme. All college students should set a goal to attain a 700 credit score prior to graduation.

Credit scores are determined by a mathematical formula used to predict the likelihood a person will default on a loan or extension of credit. The logic is that the lower the score (300-600), the higher the probability that a person will default. As credit scores increase, the likelihood of the person defaulting decreases significantly. Individuals with credit scores between 750-850 have an extremely low probability of defaulting on a loan. This is why banks and other lenders like to do business with people with high credit scores. Above-average credit scores give the lender a good indication they will recover at least the principal amount of their loan with little risk of collections activity or default.

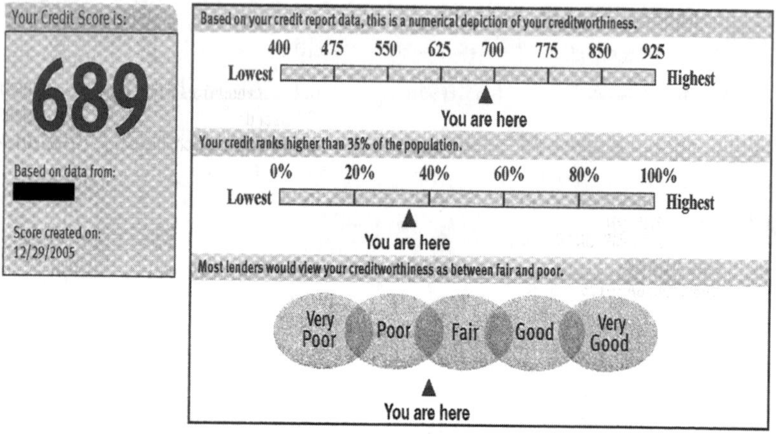

When students establish that first line of credit, their scores will typically start at about 600, which is very marginal credit, and it is up to students to build good credit histories in order to have that score increase.

Late payments are one of the worst items students can have on their credit history. Since newly established credit scores start out around 600, any late payments or negative items will cause an immediate decrease in credit score.

Conversely, payments that are made consistently on time along with decreasing outstanding debt will help increase a student's credit score. Making consistent monthly payments establishes a record of good character and will steadily decrease the amount of principal debt. Making payments by the due date and decreased balances will work together to increase scores.

DOLLARS AND SENSE

Just like low GPAs are hard to raise, once a student establishes a low credit score or bad credit, it may take several months or even years to increase his score.

When students apply for new credit, they will create what is known as an inquiry on their credit profile. If a student applies for a variety of new accounts over a period of time, the multiple credit inquiries will cause their credit score to decrease. Students should get into the habit of not applying for multiple credit items, impulsively applying for credit, or allowing potential lenders (banks, auto salesmen, credit card companies, etc.) to repeatedly pull their credit reports for review. Students must become very selective about when and by whom their credit is requested and reviewed. They should plan for circumstances that may require the application for credit. If more than one application is needed, then they all should be requested close together to minimize the impact of multiple credit inquiries.

Again, the first step is for students to learn everything they can about credit and credit scores. Students should know how to establish good financial habits and what will have a positive impact on their credit scores.

Here is a brief overview on credit scores and how they work. Credit reporting agencies use a combination of mathematical formulas known as scoring models, which take into account a number of variables to determine a person's score. There are five major categories that are primarily used to calculate a credit score:

1. **Payment history**. This is approximately 35% of the credit score. The first item any lender wants to know is whether the credit applicant has paid accounts on time. This is one of the most important factors in a credit score. Consistently paying bills by the due date shows that an individual is responsible and trustworthy with repaying debts.
2. **Outstanding debts**. 30% of the credit score is comprised of this segment. This critical category measures the total amount of outstanding debt a person has at any given time. Having a large amount of debt will negatively impact credit scores. This criterion also measures how much of a person's available credit is being used. Any time

a person uses more than 50% of their available credit, it has a negative impact on credit scores. Outstanding balances of more than 50% of the original amount also negatively impact credit scores. Whenever more than half of the available credit card limit is used, it is an indicator that the borrower may be becoming over-extended in his liabilities. A good rule of thumb is not to use more than 30% of the available credit or loan amount for any given account. When balances get close to the card limit, credit scores will decrease. Students should really develop the habit of paying off their entire credit card balances every month.

3. **Length of credit history**. This is 15% of the credit score. This item measures the length of time that credit accounts have been established. Many students have not had enough time to establish credit due to their age; therefore, this category has a big impact on their scores. Developing accounts at an early age will help to strengthen this area as students go through college. The key is to establish and maintain good credit account histories. Never close accounts after paying off the outstanding balance, because this will cause a decrease in credit scores.
4. **Application for new credit**. This is 10% of the credit score. This category measures how much new credit a person applies for over a short period, usually three to six months. Multiple applications for credit over this time will lower a credit score. Several applications for new credit over a short time will trigger a red flag with lenders who refer to this process as shopping for credit. Multiple credit inquiries or newly established accounts have a negative impact on scores. Any newly approved accounts will initially lower credit scores, then scores will begin to increase over time.

5. **Types of credit**. This is 10% of your credit score. This category measures the types of credit that are listed in a person's file. These accounts include revolving credit or installment accounts including; auto, consumer, student, and mortgage loans. The type of credit that is established in a file will have an impact on the overall score. A healthy mix of credit will have a variety of different types of accounts.

The Weather Channel

Generally, credit scores are indicators of the predictability of a person's future financial actions. The best analogy of how credit scores are determined is by comparing them to predicting the weather. If the weatherman sees a cold front approaching a warm front, he knows without a doubt that these variables will most likely produce a thunderstorm. Likewise, if an individual has had late payments, accounts in collections, and maxed-out credit cards in the past, the credit scoring model will assign a number to these variables that show lenders a financial thunderstorm is very probable. In financial terms this means more late payments, more collection accounts, foreclosures, or even bankruptcies are likely. Therefore, individuals are assigned low credit scores that alert lenders this person is a high credit risk.

A more positive forecast would apply if a person has paid his bills on time, credit card balances are at a minimum, and no negative information is contained in his credit report. This tells a potential lender that there is a "very slight chance" that this applicant would default on a loan or credit extension. When people apply for credit, the only thing lenders want to know is the probability they will get their money back. In other words, what is the financial weather going to be like in the applicant's financial future? In today's society, more products and services are being determined by an individual's credit score. Students and parents need to keep in mind there are very few numbers that are as important as their credit score. Therefore, it is imperative they understand how to develop and maintain acceptable credit scores because this single number can have a tremendous impact on their life.

Learning Points for Students and Parents

- Credit scores are determined by a mathematical formula known as a scoring model.
- Credit scores can range from 300-850.
- Employers review credit scores of potential applicants. Low scores will impact job opportunities.
- Credit scores below 600 are considered as "bad" credit.
- Credit scores beginning at 700 are considered "good" credit.
- Credit scores are related to the probability that an applicant will default on a loan or extension of credit.
- As credit scores increase, the probability of a default on a loan or extension of credit is decreased.

CHAPTER 14

The Real-Life Report Card

"Education is what remains after one has forgotten everything he learned in school."
—Albert Einstein

Report cards are issued from pre-kindergarten through the last semester at institutions of higher learning. Throughout a student's educational career, there are very few things that have more significance than the grades included in his report card. Good grades could mean rewards from parents, recognition from schools, scholarships, or even acceptance to a highly selective college/university. In contrast, bad grades could result in disciplinary actions by parents, probation at school, loss of scholarships, declined college applications, and in some cases termination of a college career. The report card is the most utilized tool to measure overall academic performance.

In the world of personal finance, the credit report is an

individual's report card. This record contains data related to a person's payment history with regards to financial obligations. Similar to a report card, the information contained in a person's credit report can be interpreted as either good or bad. Unlike report cards, many students and parents have limited knowledge about credit reports. (See Sample Credit Report in Appendix A.)

There are many credit reporting agencies, but the most widely used are known as the "big three." They are Equifax, Trans-Union, and Experian. These companies are used by lenders ninety percent of the time when information on a person's credit history is needed. Credit reporting agencies are known as repositories (storage) for the reporting of individual credit histories. Credit bureaus do not produce any information that is included in the personal credit report. They only record the historical data related to payment information that is reported to them by both public and private institutions. In addition to payment information, legal information such as judgments, liens, and bankruptcies can also be reported to credit bureaus.

Although students may not encounter these types of legal matters while in school, it is still good to be aware of what can be reported. Information contained in personal credit reports is made available to lenders as well as potential employers when an application for credit or employment is being considered.

Information is supplied to the various credit bureaus monthly. Each lender or creditor reports to the credit bureau if payments have been received as scheduled. When payments extend thirty days past the designated due date, the credit bureau is notified of this fact. Late payments are reported to the credit bureau in thirty-day increments. Payments that remain unpaid for an extended period, usually ninety to 180 days can result in being transferred to a collection agency. When accounts are transferred to collection agencies this information is noted in the credit report. Not paying financial obligations on time is one of the fastest ways to develop what is commonly known as bad credit.

When individuals pay financial obligations as scheduled, this information is also reported. On-time payments are recorded by the creditor and show in the individual's credit report as "paying as agreed." Making on-time payments is the foundation of creating a positive credit rating. This should be stressed to students as early as high school to promote the development of good credit.

Every college student should request a copy of his credit report at least every six months for review. This is one of the most vital steps in understanding credit. Reviewing credit reports help students understand how their various accounts have been reported by creditors. Unfortunately, the majority of college students will not see a copy of their credit report until they are in their late twenties or early thirties. If students really want to develop a working knowledge of credit, they need to pull their personal credit report and take time to learn how to read it. When students develop this skill, they will be able to understand which actions have the most impact on their credit score and creditworthiness. They will also be able to detect errors in their report that can be corrected to help increase their score.

DOLLARS AND SENSE

College students should request a copy of their credit report no later than the fall semester of their junior year. If there are any negative items or errors they can have them corrected prior to graduation.

Students can review their credit reports to identify areas that require improvement or patterns in their payment histories. This would be extremely valuable information for students in both undergraduate and graduate school. It would give them the ability to identify any potential problems before applying for credit or employment. If there are any deficiencies noted in their report, students can work on improving their credit, which may increase their options for employment after graduation.

Students can request a copy of their credit report online at annualcreditreport.com or call (877)322-8228. This is a free service that will provide a credit report from each of the three major credit bureaus. Depending on in which state a student has residency, he is entitled to receive a free copy of his credit report once a year, and in some states twice a year.

In addition to requesting credit reports through annual-creditreport.com, students can request a copy directly from each of the credit bureaus for a small fee—usually between $19.99 and $39.99. Another reliable website for requesting a credit report is myfico.com. It may cost an additional $5 to $10 to get a credit score with a report, but it is well worth it because students will be able to review their scores in addition to their report. It is very important that students learn how to read these reports in order to increase their overall financial literacy. It's best to learn how to interpret credit reports at a young age because this is an essential financial skill that will be used for life.

In addition to students, parents also need to develop the skill of reading a credit report. Parents will benefit by gaining insight into their own creditworthiness and will be able assist students in interpreting reports. A new trend related to college student loans involve parents being required to co-sign. Many parents may not be able to co-sign for a student loan due to bad credit. What's worst is they may not realize it until after filling out college paperwork for students. It would be more effective for parents to review their credit reports before the college application process begins. Therefore, if there are any problems identified related to their creditworthiness, they will have time to correct it.

The personal credit report is a critical tool for both students and parents. It will help to explain what is good or bad with a credit history. Unlike report cards, credit reports are an item that will be utilized to measure creditworthiness throughout the lifetime of both students and parents. Hopefully, after gaining the knowledge contained in this book, everyone will have a financial honor roll and no failing grades.

Learning Points for Students and Parents

- Credit reports contain data related to a person's payment history with regards to financial obligations.
- The three largest credit bureaus are known as The Big Three: Equifax, Trans-Union and Experian.
- Credit bureaus only store information (repository). They do not create any data included in credit reports.
- College students and parents should request a copy of their credit report every six months.
- College students and parents have to learn how to read a credit report. This is a very important life skill.
- By law, college students and parents are entitled to at least one free credit report annually.

Credit Bureau Contact Information

Equifax Credit Information Services, Inc.
P.O. Box 740241 • Atlanta, GA 30374
800-685-1111
www.equifax.com

TransUnion Consumer Soultions
P.O. Box 2000 • Chester, PA 19022-2000
877-322-8228
www.transunion.com

Experian
P.O. Box 9701 • Allen, TX 75013
800-509-8495
www.experian.com

Afterword

"Nothing in all the world is more dangerous than sincere ignorance and conscientious stupidity."
—Dr. Martin Luther King, Jr.

The above quote sums up my aim for this book perfectly. *Sincere ignorance* means that a person really just does not know about a certain topic. One of the main reasons I wrote this book is because so many students and parents really just do not have an adequate amount of knowledge on the subject of personal finance. Therefore, it is safe to say they just don't know when it comes to managing money, understanding credit, or being able to make effective investments.

It is my sincere hope that anyone who has read this book, at the very least, will realize that there is a problem with the level of financial literacy (financial education) among America's high school students, college students and their parents. I hope students will be able to identify areas where they need additional education and make a personal commitment to obtain the necessary education as soon as possible. I also want students to realize they do not have a choice whether they need to obtain this information. Every student enters the *game* of personal finance when they become young adults. This is usually between the ages of eighteen and twenty-three, and by this time, they don't have a choice in the matter.

Everything from employment opportunities to finding a suitable mate may be impacted by personal finance, including credit, money management, and investments. Therefore, I wanted to provide a resource that has the ability to guide them in their quest to understand this vital topic in America's economy. Students who choose not to become educated on this subject will continue to be prime targets for financial institutions, including banks and credit card companies. Sincere ignorance translates into increased revenues for these institutions because students do not know or understand the financial game that is being played.

The other part of this equation is the parents of high school and college students. While writing this book, I realized a profound notion regarding parents and personal finance: if parents do not understand or have a limited knowledge on this topic, there is no way they can effectively teach their children. When this gap in information occurs, students are unable to get this knowledge from their parents and will go out into world unprepared. This is why the focus of the book was expanded to include parents because if we get more parents educated, they will be in a position to pass this information on to future generations. This information, if applied correctly, has the ability to impact generations.

Increasing the knowledge base of students and parents has the potential to affect the economy on a local, state, national, and global level. This information can help to decrease the number of foreclosures, personal bankruptcies, divorces and the overall stress of making ends meet. Students will also be in a position to transition into adulthood from a financial standpoint, which will make each of them more productive citizens. In closing, remember there are three objectives this book seeks to assist every college student in achieving by the time they graduate:

1. Understand the basics of personal finance.
2. Increase financial literacy.
3. Learn how to effectively manage money and credit.

I have already started on my second book, which will go a little deeper into the world of personal finance. Now that you have the basics, it is time for a more advanced course. Thank you for allowing me to get this one book out of me. It is my sincere hope that *My College Finance* will help students and parents to develop a better understanding of personal finance in addition to avoiding the financial pitfalls of life. God bless.

Notes:

APPENDIX A

Sample Credit Report

CREDIT FILE : March 25, 2005 | **Confirmation #** 07822586

Personal Identification Information *(This section includes your name, current and previous addresses, and any other identifying information reported by your creditors.)*

Name On File: Joe Camel
Social Security # 999-99-9999 Date of Birth: 02-25-1978
Current Address: 4354 Round Tree Drive, Viking, GA 92465 Reported: 05/2000
Previous Address(es): 435 Flower Lane, Ashland, GA 25467 Reported: 04/1994
Last Reported Employment: RN: Amoco Fabrics
Previous Employment(s): RN: Smith's Plumbing

Please address all future correspondence to:

In order to speak with a Customer Service Representative regarding the specific information contained in this credit file, you must call **WITHIN 60 DAYS** of the date of this credit file **AND** have a copy of this credit file along with the confirmation number.

Credit Account Information
*(For your security, the last 4 digits of account number(s) have been replaced by *) (This section includes open and closed accounts reported by credit grantors)*

Account Column Title Descriptions:

1	Account Number - The Account number reported by credit grantor	12	Amount Past Due - The Amount Past Due as of the Date Reported
2	Date Acct. Opened - The Date that the credit grantor opened the account	13	Date of Last Paymnt - The Date of Last Payment
3	High Credit - The Highest Amount Charged	14	Actual Pay Amt - The Actual Amount of Last Payment
4	Credit Limit - The Highest Amount Permitted	15	Sched Pay Amt - The Requested Amount of Last Payment
5	Terms Duration - The Number of Installments or Payments	16	Date of Last Actvty - The Date of the Last Account Activity
6	Terms Frequency - The Scheduled Time Between Payments	17	Date Maj Delq Rptd - The Date the 1st Major Delinquency Was Reported
7	Months Reviewed - The Number of Months Reviewed	18	Charge Off Amt - The Amount Charged Off by Creditor
8	Activity Description - The Most Recent Account Activity	19	Deferred Pay Date - The 1st Payment Due Date for Deferred Loans
9	Creditor Class - The Type of Company Reporting The Account	20	Balloon Pay Amt - The Amount of Final(Balloon) Payment
10	Date Reported - The Month and Year of the Last Account Update	21	Balloon Pay Date - The Date of Final(Balloon) Payment
11	Balance Amount - The Total Amount Owed as of the Date Reported	22	Date Closed - The Date the Account was Closed

Account History Status Code Descriptions			
	1 : 30-59 Days Past Due	5 : 150-179 Days Past Due	J : Voluntary Surrender
	2 : 60-89 Days Past Due	6 : 180 or More Days Past Due	K : Repossession
	3 : 90-119 Days Past Due	G : Collection Account	L : Charge Off
	4 : 120-149 Days Past Due	H : Foreclosure	

Action Rental

Account Number (1)	Date Opened (2)	High Credit (3)	Credit Limit (4)	Terms Duration (5)	Terms Frequency (6)	Mnths Revd (7)	Activity Description (8)	Creditor Clasification (9)
777111	11/2003	$4,228		15 Months	Monthly	15	Paid and Closed	

Items As of Date Reported (10)	Balance Amount (11)	Amount Past Due (12)	Date of Last Paymnt (13)	Actual Paymnt Amount (14)	Scheduled Paymnt Amount (15)	Date of Last Activity (16)	Date Maj. Del. 1st Rptd (17)	Charge Off Amount (18)	Deferred Pay Start Date (19)	Balloon Pay Amount (20)	Balloon Pay Date (21)	Date Closed (22)
02/2005	$0		02/2005	$308	$306	02/2005						02/2005

Current Status - Pays As Agreed; Type of Account - Installment; Type of Loan - Business Loan - Individual Is Personally Liable; Whose Account - Joint Account;

Best Warehouse

Account Number	Date Opened	High Credit	Credit Limit	Terms Duration	Terms Frequency	Mnths Revd	Activity Description	Creditor Clasification
1112225	11/1998						Paid	

Items As of Date Reported	Balance Amount	Amount Past Due	Date of Last Paymnt	Actual Paymnt Amount	Scheduled Paymnt Amount	Date of Last Activity	Date Maj. Del. 1st Rptd	Charge Off Amount	Deferred Pay Start Date	Balloon Pay Amount	Balloon Pay Date	Date Closed
01/2005	$711				$35.00	01/2001						

Current Status - Charge Off; Type of Account - Revolving; Type of Loan - Credit Card; Whose Account - Individual Account; ADDITIONAL INFORMATION - Settlement Accepted on This Account;

Chewbacca

Account Number	Date Opened	High Credit	Credit Limit	Terms Duration	Terms Frequency	Mnths Revd	Activity Description	Creditor Clasification
2001246	12/1996					73		

Items As of Date Reported	Balance Amount	Amount Past Due	Date of Last Paymnt	Actual Paymnt Amount	Scheduled Paymnt Amount	Date of Last Activity	Date Maj. Del. 1st Rptd	Charge Off Amount	Deferred Pay Start Date	Balloon Pay Amount	Balloon Pay Date	Date Closed
03/2005	$2335				$68.00	03/2005						

Current Status - Pays As Agreed; Type of Account - Revolving; Type of Loan - Charge Account; Whose Account - Individual Account;

Account History with Status Codes	06/2002	01/2002	10/2001	05/2001	01/2001	07/2000	01/2000
	1	1	1	1	1	1	1

Creekside Community Bank

Account Number	Date Opened	High Credit	Credit Limit	Terms Duration	Terms Frequency	Mnths Revd	Activity Description	Creditor Clasification
311774599	11/1996		$710			58		

Items As of Date Reported	Balance Amount	Amount Past Due	Date of Last Paymnt	Actual Paymnt Amount	Scheduled Paymnt Amount	Date of Last Activity	Date Maj. Del. 1st Rptd	Charge Off Amount	Deferred Pay Start Date	Balloon Pay Amount	Balloon Pay Date	Date Closed
12/2003	$4278				$145.00	12/2003						

Current Status - Pays As Agreed; Type of Account - Revolving; Type of Loan - Charge Account; Whose Account - Individual Account;

Account History with Status Codes	06/2002	02/2002	01/2002	11/2001	10/2001	05/2001	01/2000
	1	1	1	2	1	1	1

J&L Investment & Loan

Account Number	Date Opened	High Credit	Credit Limit	Terms Duration	Terms Frequency	Mnths Revd	Activity Description	Creditor Clasification
40007925	10/2003	$15,574		181 Months		15	Paid and Closed	

Items As of Date Reported	Balance Amount	Amount Past Due	Date of Last Paymnt	Actual Paymnt Amount	Scheduled Paymnt Amount	Date of Last Activity	Date Maj. Del. 1st Rptd	Charge Off Amount	Deferred Pay Start Date	Balloon Pay Amount	Balloon Pay Date	Date Closed
01/2005	$6735				$250	01/2005						

Current Status - Pays As Agreed; Type of Account - Installment; Type of Loan - Partially Secured; Whose Account - Individual Account;

Discount Wholesale

Account Number	Date Opened	High Credit	Credit Limit	Terms Duration	Terms Frequency	Mnths Revd	Activity Description	Creditor Clasification
548796245	10/2004	$19,613		48 Months	Monthly	4		

Items As of Date Reported	Balance Amount	Amount Past Due	Date of Last Paymnt	Actual Paymnt Amount	Scheduled Paymnt Amount	Date of Last Activity	Date Maj. Del. 1st Rptd	Charge Off Amount	Deferred Pay Start Date	Balloon Pay Amount	Balloon Pay Date	Date Closed
02/2005	$18,251		02/2005		$490	02/2005						

Current Status - Pays As Agreed; Type of Account - Installment; Type of Loan - Auto; Whose Account - Individual Account;

Capital Two

Account Number	Date Opened	High Credit	Credit Limit	Terms Duration	Terms Frequency	Mnths Revd	Activity Description	Creditor Clasification
122334982	10/2000	$8,100		120 Months	Monthly	35	Paid	

Items As of Date Reported	Balance Amount	Amount Past Due	Date of Last Paymnt	Actual Paymnt Amount	Scheduled Paymnt Amount	Date of Last Activity	Date Maj. Del. 1st Rptd	Charge Off Amount	Deferred Pay Start Date	Balloon Pay Amount	Balloon Pay Date	Date Closed
06/2004	$1695				$78.00	09/2003						10/2003

Current Status - Pays As Agreed; Type of Account - Installment; Type of Loan - Secured; Whose Account - Individual Account; ADDITIONAL INFORMATION - Account Paid/Zero Balance; Account Paid/Zero Balance; Secured;

APPENDIX B

Suggested Reading List

- The Holy Bible
- *The Art of War* by Sun Tzu
- *The Automatic Millionaire* by David Bach
- *The Billion Dollar BET* by Robert Johnson
- *Black Enterprise* magazine
- *The Credit Card Catastrophe* by Matty Simmons
- *Forbes*
- *Fortune*
- *The Making of a Blockbuster* by Gail DeGeorge
- *The Millionaire Next Door* by Thomas J. Stanley / William D. Danko
- *Multiple Streams of Income* by Robert Allen
- *The 9 Steps to Financial Freedom* by Suze Orman
- *Rich Dad Poor Dad* by Robert Kiyosaki
- *The Richest Man in Babylon* by George S. Clason
- *Smart Money Moves For African Americans* by Kelvin Boston
- *Think and Grow Rich* by Napoleon Hill
- *Think and Grow Rich: A Black Choice* by Dennis Kimbro
- *Unlimited Power* by Anthony Robbins
- *Unlocking Wealth* by Robert Wilson
- *The Wall Street Journal*
- *Why Should White Guys Have All the Fun?* by Reginald F. Lewis / Blair S. Walker
- *Why We Want You To Be Rich* by Donald J. Trump / Robert Kiyosaki

Notes:

APPENDIX C

Credit Resources/Helpful Web Sites

www.mycollegefinance.com

Equifax: (800) 685-1111
www.equifax.com

Experian: (888) 397-3742
www.experian.com

Trans-Union: (800) 888-4213
www.transunion.com

Annual Credit Report: (877) 322-8228
www.annualcreditreport.com

My Fico: www.myfico.com

Bankrate: www.Bankrate.com

Jump$tart: www.jumpstart.org

MSN Money: www.moneycentral.msn.com

Wall Street Journal College Journal: www.collegejournal.com

Card Web: www.cardweb.com

Notes:

APPENDIX D

The Fine Print

This is the section of the credit card agreement most people neglet to read, but it's the most important part.

IMPORTANT INFORMATION REGARDING YOUR APPLICATION

Annual percentage rate for purchases	Other APRs	Variable rate information	Grace period for repayment of the balance for purchases	Method of computing the balances for purchases	Annual Fee	Minimum finance charge
• 0% introductory Annual Percentage Rate on purchases for the first twelve months of Cardmembership, then your APR will be a variable rate equal to 8.25%, up to 18.24%, as determined by us based on our credit evaluation and a number of factors, including size of the credit line.	• **Balance Transfer APR:** 7.99% fixed for the life of the transferred balance, but only if transfer is made during the first six months as a Cardmember. Then the Standard APR for Purchases will apply. • **Cash Advance APR:** 23.24%. • **Default APR:** 24.24% (30.24% for Cash Advances) on defaulted accounts, or 30.24% on all balances for seriously defaulted accounts; see explanation below.†	• Your APRs may vary. The APRs for purchases are determined for each billing period by adding 0.00%, 3.99%, 6.99%, or 9.99% to the Prime Rate. The APRs for cash advances, defaulted accounts and seriously defaulted accounts are determined for each billing period by adding 14.99%, 15.99% and 21.99% respectively, to the Prime Rate.§	• 25 days for purchases, if the previous balance shown on each billing statement is paid in full by each respective due date.	• Average daily balance (including new purchases).	• None	• $0.50

Other Fees: Late Payment Fee: $19 on balances less than $400 and $38 on balances $400 or greater. Over limit Fee: $35. Balance transfer fee: There is no balance transfer transaction fee associated with this offer. However, future balance transfers may incur a fee as disclosed at the time of the applicable offer or transaction. Fee for Cash Advances: 3% of each transaction with a $5 minimum and no maximum.

Patriot Act Notice: Federal law requires all financial institutions to obtain, verify and record information that identifies each person who opens an account, including your name, address, date of birth, and other information that will allow us to verify your identity.

SOLICITATION DISCLOSURES

As required by law, the rates, fees and other costs of this credit offer are disclosed below. The Cardmember Agreement sets forth all Account terms and will be sent with the card. Account terms may change. We have the right to change your APRs, fees, and other terms at any time, for any reason including, but not limited to, any change in your credit history, credit obligations, account performance, use of your credit lines with us or any creditor, or our financial return. Any changes will be in accordance with your Cardmember Agreement and applicable law.

All information is accurate as of 2/28/07.

Annual Percentage Rate (APR) for Purchases	An Introductory APR of 0% will apply for the first 12 billing cycles of your Account.[1] After that, a variable Customary APR of **14.99%**[2] will apply. (Minimum Customary APR: 14.99%.)
Annual Percentage Rate (APR) for Balance Transfers	An Introductory APR of 0% will apply for the first 12 billing cycles of your Account.[1] After that, a variable Customary APR of 14.99%[2] will apply.
Other APRs	Variable Cash APR: 25.15%.[3] (Minimum Cash APR: 20.90%.) Variable Default APR: 30.49%.[4] (Minimum Default APR: 29.49%.)
Variable Rate Information	Your APRs may vary. The rates are determined monthly by adding the Index (described below) and: • 6.74% ("Spread") for the Customary APR for credit card purchases and balance transfers. • 16.90% ("Spread") for the Cash APR for cash advances, including cash advances made by credit card check. • 22.24% ("Spread") for the Default APR. For each billing cycle, the Index is determined in the month prior to the month in which the billing cycle ends. In that prior month, the highest (U.S.) "Prime Rate" published in the Money Rates table of *The Wall Street Journal* is selected (the "Index"). If the Index has changed, the new variable rates will take effect with the billing cycle that ends on or after the first day of the month following the Index change.
Grace Period for Repayment of Balance for Purchases	You have at least 20 days from the date of the periodic statement to avoid a Finance Charge on new credit card purchases, provided you paid your previous balance in full.
Method of Computing the Balance for Purchases	Average Daily Balance (including new purchases).
Annual Fee	None
Minimum Finance Charge	$2.00 for each billing cycle in which a Periodic Finance Charge is payable.
Foreign Transaction Fee	1% of the U.S. dollar amount will apply to transactions made in a foreign currency.

Cash Advance Fee: 3% on balance transfers, any advance by credit card check, through the ATM or over the counter ($10 minimum); 5% on all other cash advances ($20 minimum); unless otherwise disclosed. Finance Charges accrue from the date of transaction. Cash advances will be limited. Your cash advance limit is disclosed on your billing statement.

Balance transfer checks will be limited. Balance transfers may not be used to make payments on any Beneficial or HSBC credit card, including any GM Card, Corvette® MasterCard®, Union Plus® Credit Card, Household Bank® or Orchard Bank® Credit Card, or to pay a loan made by any other HFC, Beneficial or HSBC company.

Glossary

The following terms were included for students and parents. Although all of these terms were not used in this book, they have been included to assist readers in expanding their vocabulary related to personal finance.

"A" Loan: offered to individuals who have demonstrated a good credit history. They have the best possible terms and conditions, including the best interest rate available.

Amortization: The repayment schedule of fixed payments over a predetermined period. Each payment includes part of the principal balance and the interest charged; usually seen with mortgages and car loan payments.

Annual Fee: Once-a-year charge by credit card companies for the use of their card. This payment is in addition to interest charges, over-the-limit fees, and charges related to cash advances.

Appreciation: Increase in the market value of real estate related to home improvements or a change in market conditions.

APR: Annual Percentage Rate; the cost of credit expressed as an annual rate. Interest applied to credit based on a twelve-month period.

ATM: Automated teller machine; individual electronic teller machines used to dispense money, make deposits, check balances or transfer money between accounts.

"B" or "C" Loan: Offered to individuals with negative credit histories. These loans do not have the best possible terms and conditions or the best interest rates. They typically have higher interest rates.

Bad Credit: Negative credit history that is reflected in a credit report. This includes late or missed payments, collection accounts, defaulted student loans, legal items (judgments, liens, or bankruptcy) or other items viewed as negative by creditors. Credit scores are 600 or less.

Bad Debt: Loans or debts that have gone unpaid for an extended period. These accounts are typically transferred to collection agencies to attempt to collect the unpaid balances.

Bankruptcy: Legal process that individuals go through when they are unable to pay their debts. The most common types are Chapter 7 and Chapter 13. In Chapter 7, the debtor's assets are sold or liquidated to cover debts. Any remaining debts are forgiven or discharged. In Chapter 13, the bankruptcy court sets up an acceptable plan for the individual to repay debts.

Borrower: An individual, group, or company who has been given money or funds for personal or business use.

Bounced Check: This occurs when payment is returned or dishonored by a bank due to lack of money required to complete transaction; also known as Insufficient Funds or NSF.

Budget: Worksheet that lists all of a person's actual or potential expenses and income; a worksheet that shows the plans for income and expenses related to re-paying debts, savings, and investments.

Capacity: A potential borrower's ability to demonstrate to a lending institution he has sufficient income to repay a loan.

Capital: Cash, investments, or assets possessed by an individual; the amount of money or investment needed for a business project.

Cash Reserves: Money, investments, and liquid assets available to an individual; money that has been set aside to be used for unforeseen financial obligations.

Charge Card: Account that requires credit purchases to be paid in full at the end of the month. There is no option to carry balances over to the next month. No interest is charged on these accounts; an example is the traditional American Express card.

Charge-offs: Loans or debts that have gone unpaid for an extended period, usually ninety to 180 days; accounts that the original creditor has given up on collecting. This information is reported to the credit bureau and inserted in the individual's credit report.

Cosigner: A person who accepts equal credit and payment responsibility in the establishment of a new loan or credit account; typically required when the primary borrower has compromised or negative credit. If the primary borrower fails to make payments as scheduled, negative credit reporting is reported for both parties.

Collateral: Real or perceived value of personal property used to secure a loan. If the borrower defaults on the loan, the lender takes possession of the property to satisfy the debt.

Collection Accounts: Past-due bills or debts that a creditor transfers to a collection agency for the purpose of retrieving outstanding debt; they are reported on the borrower's credit report.

Credit: A financial agreement to pay for goods or services over a specified period of time; can be used via cards, personal or auto loans, or mortgages.

Credit Bureau: Companies that collect and store information on an individual's payment history, which is developed into reports that are sold to companies responsible for processing loan or employment applications; the big three credit bureaus are Equifax, Experian, and Trans-Union.

Credit Card: Used to make purchases at various retailers. The charges are revolving and most balances are carried over each month with interest charged on the unpaid balances. There is a predetermined amount allowed for purchases known as the credit limit.

Credit Grantor: Responsible for approving extension of credit or approval of loans.

Credit History: Record of how an individual has re-paid his debts. This information is reported in thirty-day increments included in a consumer's credit report.

Credit Repair Companies: For-profit companies that promise to restore good credit to individuals who have a negative history. Service is done for a fee that is charged to the client.

Credit Report: A detailed document that contains information related to a person's repayment history of various debts, including revolving credit, installment loans, and secured debts; they give information on payment histories in thirty-day intervals.

Credit Reporting Agency: See Credit Bureau.

Credit Risk: Related to the likelihood of default by a potential borrower.

Credit Score: A statistical number that is derived by various scoring models, which is a prediction of potential future default based on prior payment history.

Credit Scoring Models: A combination of mathematical formulas and variables used to determine a person's credit rating. Bureaus have different models, therefore actual ratings from each company may vary.

Creditor: A person or entity to whom money is owed.

Creditworthiness: A measure of whether a person has established a positive credit and payment history over a period of time.

Deadbeat: Term used by credit card industry to describe consumers who pay their revolving credit card purchases in full every month to avoid paying any interest on their accounts. Company profits are decreased when interest is not paid on accounts.

Debit Card: Used to make credit purchases through the use of money in a checking account. In addition to credit purchases, it can be used to make electronic purchases or payments. It can also be used to access money via automated teller machines; also known as check cards.

Debt-to-Income Ratio: A mathematical formula where a person's debts are divided by his income. The resulting percentage is used by lenders to determine how much of a person's current income is obligated to his current debt. The higher the ratio, the more income is needed to satisfy payment of debts.

Debtor: Borrower.

Deficit: Expenses are more than income; occurs when there is a shortage of money available to pay bills or obligations.

Default: Failure to make payments according to borrower's agreement; reported to credit bureaus to be added to credit reports.

Default Rate: An increase in the interest rate due to one or more missed payments. Some credit cards have low or fixed interest rates such as 9.99% APR, but these rates can increase to as much as 29.99% when payments are missed.

Direct Deposit: Process employers use to automatically enter payroll checks into an employee's checking account. Employees who set up direct deposit do not have to cash their payroll checks because the funds are electronically transferred to their checking or savings account.

EFT: Electronic Funds Transfer: The movement of money from checking or savings accounts to automated teller machines ATM), card payment terminals, and electronic payments for purchases or bill payments.

Equity: Increased value of real property that is created by property appreciation and by reducing the outstanding principal of a house, condo or town house; can be converted to cash profits once the property is sold.

Expenses: Financial obligations; examples are monthly bills, credit card payments, tuition or loan payments.

Finance Charge: The cost for the use of loan or credit services.

Financial Literacy: Individual's level of knowledge related to credit, banking, money management, and personal finance.

Fixed Expenses: Financial obligations that have payment amounts that remain unchanged each month; Examples are student loans, car payments, rent/mortgage, or home insurance.

Foreclosure: Legal process where a home is sold by the bank due to the borrower's failure to make mortgage payments.

Foreign ATM Fee: A charge, usually $1.50 to $3, applied when customers use an ATM outside their bank's approved network. The actual ATM used will also have a charge for customers who are not a part of their banking network, so customers who use these machines will have two different charges.

Good Credit: Term used to describe an individual who has made payments on time and has managed his credit history responsibly. Some industry professionals consider good credit as a score of 700-plus.

Gross Income: The total amount of compensation (money) received before any deductions are taken out.

Helicopter Parents: People who are constantly hovering over the lives of their young-adult children; many of these people are part of the Baby Boomer generation and are very involved in matters related to their young-adult children.

Income: Term used to represent money that is generated by an individual either through employment or investments.

Inquiry: A creditor's request for a copy of an individual's credit report; each one is noted on a person's report; too many can have a negative effect on a person's credit history.

Installment Account: The consumer agrees to make fixed payments over a specified period; examples include personal loans, auto loans, or jewelry store accounts.

Insufficient Funds: See Bounced Check.

Insufficient Funds Fee: A bank charge to customers who have bounced checks or NSF. When a check is dishonored or returned by a bank due to lack of funds, a fee is charged to the customer's checking account.

Interest: A charge for the use of a lender's funds or extension of credit; additional funds generated from an individual's personal investments.

Interest-Only Payments: Money that does not decrease the principal or original loan amount; all the money is applied toward the interest charged on a loan.

Introductory Rate Period: A specific amount of time, at the beginning of a credit card agreement where there is no interest or a low interest rate. Interest rates can increase at the end of the period (see Jump Rate) or it can increase if there is a missed payment (see Default Rate).

Joint Accounts: A financial agreement established by two or more people; each person is equally responsible and accountable according to the contractual terms. The account's history is reported on the credit report of each person designated as an authorized user.

Jump Rate: When the introductory period ends for new credit cards the interest rate charged typically increases to a higher rate (e.g., Six-month introductory rate of 9.99% increases to 23.99%).

Late Fee: A charge applied to a borrower's account when payments are not made on time.

Late Payments: Money sent to lender that is received after the due date set by the lender; late payments are one of the most damaging items on a person's credit history.

Lender: See Creditor.

Line of Credit: An authorized amount of money granted to an individual; usually secured by either personal or business assets.

Money Management: Ability to consistently and effectively plan the use of income to satisfy financial liabilities or obligations to create wealth opportunities. This includes checking, savings, and investment accounts.

Mortgage: A loan that is related to the purchase of real estate; also grants legal permission to the lender to repossess the purchased real estate if the buyer fails to make loan payments in a timely manner.

Needs: Items that are required or necessary for survival; three basics are food, clothing, and shelter.

Net Income: Amount of pay that remains after all deductions have been removed; take-home pay.

NSF: See Bounced Checks.

Over-the-limit fee: A charge that is applied to accounts for exceeding the limit on a credit card account.

Outstanding Checks: Items that have not been processed against available money in a checking account. Once an item has been processed, the money is removed from the checking account.

Payment Due Date: Specified deadline for creditors or lenders to receive money for an outstanding financial obligation; money received after this time can be subject to additional fees (late fees) and negative reporting to the credit bureaus.

Personal Loan: Agreement to borrow money for any reason other than for business use.

PIN: Personal identification number: Used as a security feature in the processing of ATM or other financial transactions.

Predatory Lending: Creditors who use excessive interest charges, including deceptive contract language, to take advantage of unsuspecting customers. The most notable examples of predatory lending are related to real estate transactions.

Pre-Payment Penalty: Charges related to repaying a loan earlier than the scheduled pay-off date.

Principal: The original amount of money or credit borrowed by an individual; full repayment of a loan is not achieved until the balance has been paid in full.

Revolver: Customers who carry credit card balances month to month. It is estimated that 65% (fifty-one million) of all customers with credit cards carry a balance month to month.

Revolving Account: Allows an individual the option to pay charges in full or make minimum monthly payments on the outstanding balance and carry the balance to the next month; the best example is a credit card.

Revolving Debt: Accumulated financial liabilities or expenses that are not paid in full each month; includes credit cards, personal loans, or lines of credit.

Savings: Money placed into an account that accumulates interest; funds available for long-term financial goals, not intended for daily living expenses.

Secured Credit Card: Requires potential users to pay a monthly fee in order to use the card; users are sometimes required to actually make a deposit that is held as collateral.

Shopping: Term used to describe consumers who open multiple credit card accounts over a short period; this causes credit scores to decrease, because each time a new credit card account is opened consumers lose points initially. When multiple accounts are opened more points are lost.

Student Loans: Public, federal, or private lending to pay for college tuition, books, and fees. Sallie Mae is the largest lender of student loans in the United States.

Sub-prime: Loans or financial products that are designed and utilized by consumers with negative credit histories or low credit scores. These products have high interest rates due to the increased risk of default by borrowers.

Surplus: Income exceeds expenses; occurs when there is money remaining after all obligations have been paid.

Universal Default: Clause within credit card contract that allows an issuer to increase the interest rate on accounts if the borrower makes a late payment on any open account, which could cause a decrease in the borrower's credit score. Example: if a person makes one late payment on his car loan, the interest rate can be increased on his credit card account. Credit card issuers feel the late payment shows that the person is more of a credit risk due to the one late payment.

Unsecured Debt: Loans or extensions of credit that are not secured or collateralized.

Variable Expenses: Financial obligations that may change from month to month. Examples include cell phone, long-distance, or grocery bills.

Wants: Non-essential items for daily living.

Withdrawal: Removal of funds from checking, savings, or investment accounts.

Notes:

About the Author

Joaquin Thompson is a graduate of Howard University. He has several years of experience as a speaker, writer, and educator on the topic of personal finance. He is the founder of mycollegefinance.com, the premiere website for students and their parents to get information on credit cards, money management strategies, and investing. He has also been featured in *BusinessWeek* magazine.

INDEX

D

R

S

T

U

V

W

Additional Book Services

To order additional copies of this book visit the website www.gorillapublishing.org or www.mycollegefinance.com

Quality discounts are available on this book for sales promotions, premiums, fundraising or educational use. For information contact, Gorilla Publishing, 1025 Veterans Memorial Highway., Suite 310-229, Mableton, Georgia 30126. Phone 404-993-3445

All schools, Public and Private will receive a special bulk rate up to 40% off retail price based on volume. Schools /school groups can also receive profits up to $5.00 per unit sold during fundraising campaigns. This is a great opportunity for schools / school groups to educate students about personal finance and raise needed funds simultaneously. For more information email us at schoolsales@gorillapublishing.org .

Seminars, workshops and presentations related to this book and the topic of personal finance are available for schools, businesses, churches and any other organizations. Please contact Gorilla publishing for available dates and times.

Gorilla Publishing
1025 Veterans Memorial Highway, Suite 310-229
Mableton, GA 30126

Phone: 404-993-3445

Special Thanks

The Amazing Cakes Bakery